Black Historical Figures

COMEDIANS

Copyright © 2022 by Every Dollar Countz LLC
All rights reserved. This book or any portion thereof
may not be reproduced or used in any manner whatsoever
without the express written permission of the publisher
except for the use of brief quotations in a book review.

TABLE OF CONTENTS

43 DAVE CHAPPELLE

179 KEVIN HART

67 SHERYL UNDERWOOD

3 Loretta Mary Aiken	67 Sheryl Underwood	131 Cedric Kyles
11 Bernard McCullough	75 Richard Gregory	139 Tiffany Haddish
19 Wanda Sykes	83 Robert Townsend	147 Keenen Ivory Wayans
27 Edward Murphy	91 Lori Rambough	155 Arsenio Hall
35 Whoopi Goldberg	99 Steve Harvey	163 Annette Jones
43 Dave Chappelle	107 Broderick Smiley	171 Martin Lawrence
51 LaWanda Page	115 Monique Hicks	179 Kevin Hart
59 John Sanford	123 Richard Pryor	187 Jordan Peele
		195 Christopher Rock

These Workbooks are geared to intrigue, inspire and motivate you to want to learn more about these Black Historical Figures(BHFs) and others. Also to do more research on your own. We know this isn't all the history of these individuals. We want you to do some of the research also. We try to be as accurate as possible during our research. If there are some stories or questions that aren't as stated, please contact us at info@wegonnalearntoday.com.

Loretta Mary Aiken

Loretta Mary Aiken

MARCH 19, 1894 – MAY 23, 1975
COMEDIAN/ACTRESS

LEFT BLANK ON PURPOSE

Loretta Mary Aiken

Loretta Mary Aiken

Loretta Mary Aiken

Loretta Mary Aiken

Loretta Mary Aiken

Loretta Mary Aiken

Directions: read the bio below and answer the following questions.

Hi, my name is Loretta Mary Aiken. I was born on March 19, 1894, in Brevard, NC. At the age of 14, I started traveling with a vaudeville-style minstrel show that starred Butterbeans and Susie. I sang and entertained people. I got my stage name, "Jackie Mabley," from an old boyfriend and due to the maternal role that I played for other comedians on the circuit, I was known as Jackie "Moms" Mabley. I made my debut at Connie's Inn in Harlem. I was one of the most successful entertainers on the Chitlin' Circuit. Due to my non-threatening image, I was able to address topics that were too edgy for most comics of the time, including racism, sexuality and having children after becoming a widow. In 1962, I performed at Carnegie Hall, which brought more white people into my audience. I also had multiple TV appearances on The Smothers Brothers Comedy Hour, The Bill Cosby Show, The Pearl Bailey Show, The Apollo Theater and The Ed Sullivan Show, to name a few.

1. Where did I perform when I started?
    A. Vaudeville-style minstrel show
    B. The Pearl Bailey Show
    C. The Bill Cosby show
2. What year did I perform at the Carnegie Hall?
    A. 1960
    B. 1961
    C. 1962
3. What name did I acquire as I kept performing?
    A. Jackie Mabley
    B. Jackie "Moms" Mabley
    C. Jackie

Directions: Answer the questions to solve the crossword puzzle. You can use the internet if you get stuck on any question.

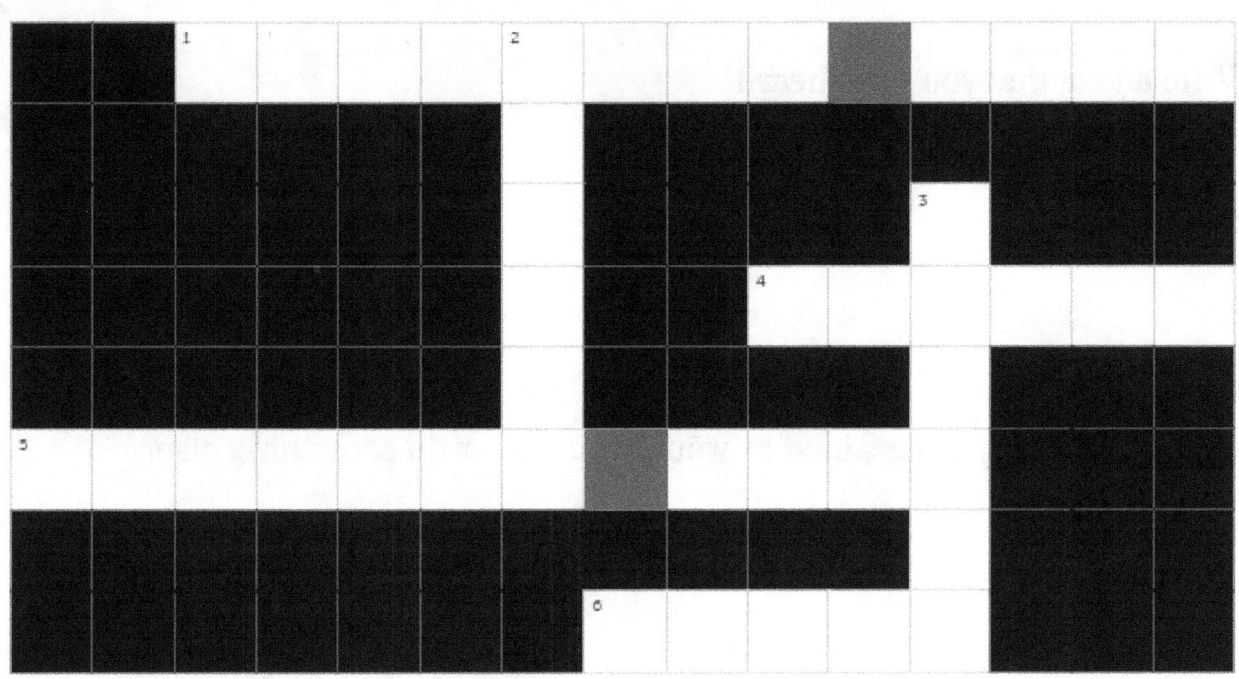

Across

1) Moms Mabley was the first women comedian to headline _____ in 1962.

4) Moms Mabley was the first woman comic to performe at the ____ in 1930.

5) Moms Mabley was the oldest person at _____ to have a Top 40 Hit with "Abraham, Martin and John."

6) Moms Mabley's comedy career spanned over ___ years.

Down

2) Moms Mabley stared in the film "Amazing Grace," she was ____ years old.

3) Moms Mabley recorded over twenty _____ albums during the last half of her career.

Directions: Read and answer the questions. These are your opinions so the answers will vary.

Write a joke that you have heard?

Do you like being entertained or would you rather do something else?

Who is the funniest classmate in this classroom?

Directions: Unscramble the words below about Moms Mabley. See if you can get the bonus word.

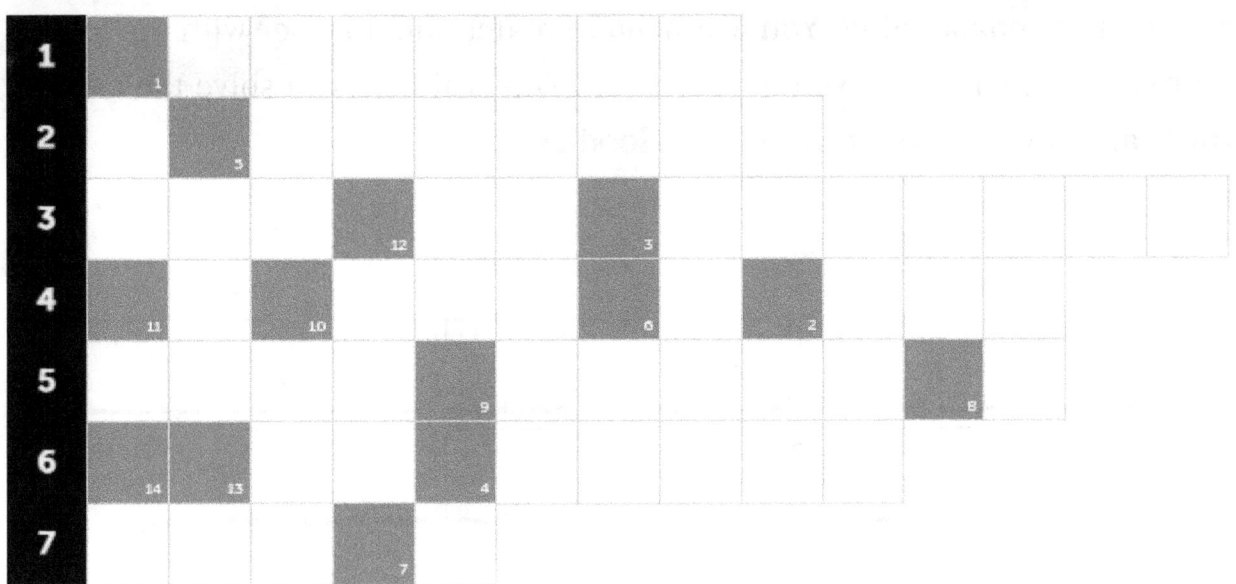

BONUS WORD

1	2	3	4	5	6	7

8	9	10	11	12	13	14

Unscramble Words

1) miaoecdn   **2)** denlalecv   **3)** uewohsinldalsv
4) naecglherlai   **5)** agzeagrcanim   **6)** euarnttrin
7) ybone

Directions: This is the WGLT Challenge. Solve the cryptogram. As the puzzle solver, you need to find which number belongs to which character. And this can be pretty challenging! You will need to match the number with the letter. There are some letters given to you below. This will help you solve the other words and unlock more characters. **Good Luck.**

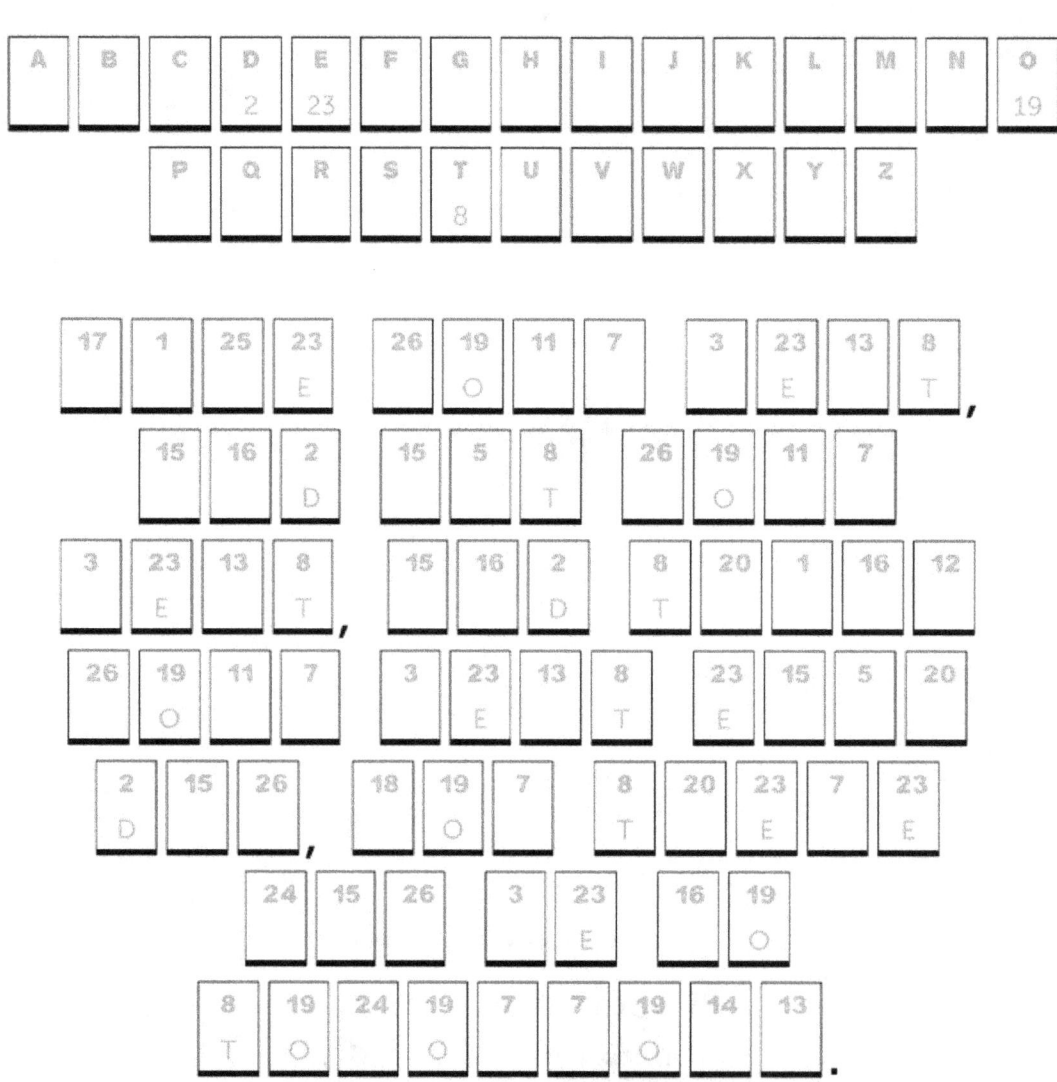

Bernard McCullough

Bernard McCullough

October 5, 1957 – August 9, 2008
COMEDIAN / ACTOR

11

LEFT BLANK ON PURPOSE

Bernard McCullough

Bernard McCullough

Bernard McCullough

Bernard McCullough

Bernard McCullough

Bernard McCullough

Directions: read the bio below and answer the following questions.

Hi, my name is Bernard Jeffrey McCullough. I was born on October 5, 1957, in Chicago, IL. I graduated from Chicago Vocational High School. I became a professional comedian at the age of 19. In 1977, I was on the road 47 weeks out of the year performing comedy. I performed in Chicago parks to the Chicago's Regal Theater, as well as other comedy clubs. My performance at "HBO's Def Comedy Jam" gave me a big boost in the mainstream industry. In 1992, I made my film debut in "Mo' Money". In 1995, I played Pastor Clever in the film Friday. In 1999, I played Jangle Lang in the film Life. In 2001, I starred in my own TV show: "The Bernie Mac Show". The show lasted five years and consisted of over one hundred episodes. Some more of the shows, films and TV that I have done include "The Kings of Comedy", "Ocean's Eleven", "Moesha", "Charlie's Angels: Full Throttle", "The Wayans Bros", "Madagascar: Escape 2 Africa" and "Saturday Night Live".

1. What was the name of my High School?
    A. Jesuit High School
    B. Lindblom Math & Science Academy High School
    C. Chicago Vocational High School
2. What year did I start doing comedy?
    A. 1979
    B. 1977
    C. 1999
3. I made my breakthrough doing what show?
    A. HBO's Def Comedy Jam
    B. The Apollo
    C. Chicago Regal Theatre

Directions: find the words associated with Bernie Mac's life and career.

```
V W O Y D U A Y U J U K Y E W S F F
T H E P L A Y E R S C L U B Z K A O
G K S Q J C Z A B J W C V Z Q Q Y H
L L T R A N S F O R M E R S J J Y R
F S X N Z L Q M K J H 3 V J C P X Z
W G M T A K I A K U Y J N P T M G Q
O J E L C O W G I T Q Y N L V T N P
H C N T T Y V D R V J E F O U N T H
S J V R O C J A B V A J T G P G H X
C K V E R T P A C M I T Q A Z T G Z
A O C L W E X Y O O J Q A C E S D C
M Q C U S Y C E M B H W L I N H Z Y
E I I U X A X N E M J M F H Q E Q D
I L O W V D Z O D Q L R B C K A T F
N H Y S Q I W M I Y A T N A S D A B
R A K V S R E - A F Y Y C L O N Q Y
E W B I D F M O N I L O J S J V T A
B K O N M K E M S F B A X W A N A K
```

Find These Words

HOUSEPARTY3　　ACTOR　　　　　　THEPLAYERSCLUB
COMEDIAN　　　　TRANSFORMERS　FRIDAY
BERNIEMACSHOW　CHICAGO　　　　MO-MONEY
BADSANTA

Directions: read and answer the questions. These are your opinions so the answers will vary.

Would you be able to stand in front of people and tell jokes? Why or Why not?

_____

_____

If you became a star, would you change your name? If yes what would it be.

_____

_____

Would you be able to be away from your family for a long time?

_____

_____

_____

_____

Directions: read and answer the questions below. There are clues in the puzzle to help you. Try and solve the cryptic message.

Clue for cryptic message: Bernie Mac did this for a living.

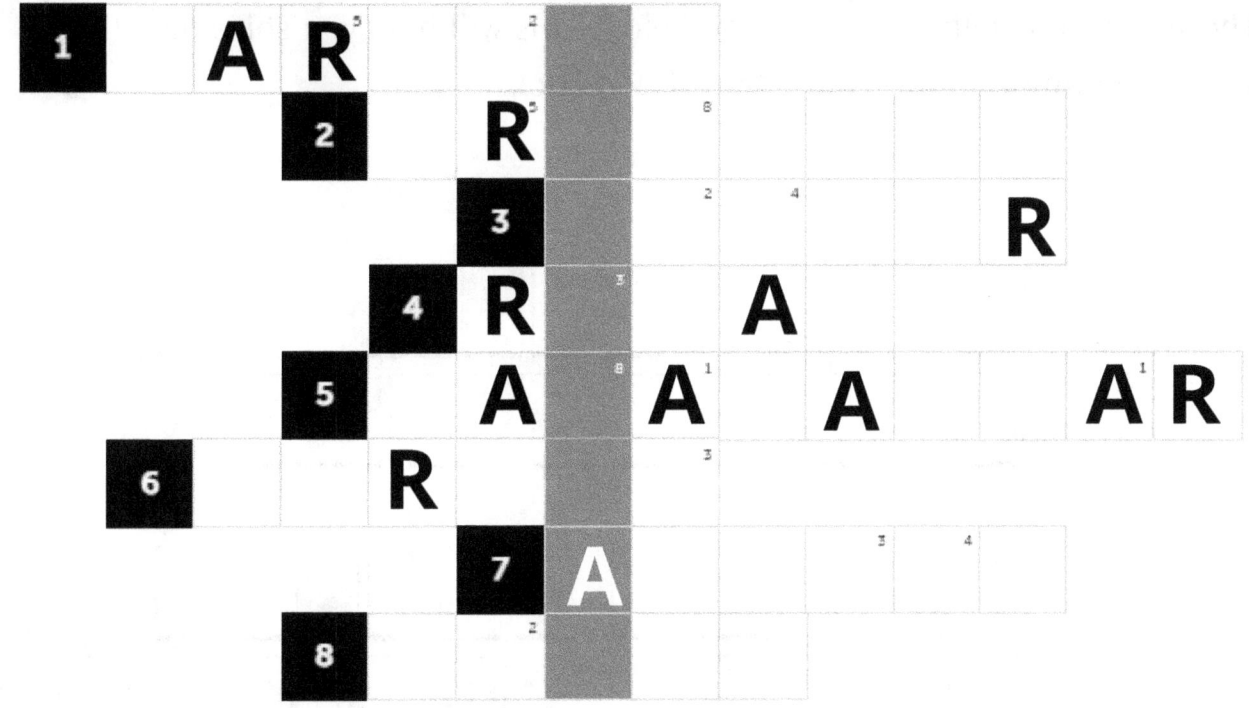

Questions

1) Bernie Mac use to be the opening act for Redd Foxx, Dionne ____ and Natalie Cole to name a few.

2) Bernie Mac ____ and starred in the comedy act "Who Ya Wit Tour."

3) Bernie Mac was thirty-two when he won the ___ Lite Comedy Search.

4) Bernie Mac use to perform at the famous '__ Theatre' in Chicago.

5) Bernie Mac was the voice of Zuba, the Lion's long-lost father in _____: Escape 2 Africa.

6) Bernie Mac had his own sitcom called 'The ____ Mac Show', which ran for five years.

7) Bernie Mac was Bosley in the comedy sequel "Charlie's ____: Full Throttle."

8) Bernie Mac was one of the four comedians on the "The ____ of Comedy" tour.

17

Directions: This is the WGLT Challenge. Solve the cryptogram. As the puzzle solver, you need to find which number belongs to which character. And this can be pretty challenging! You will need to match the number with the letter. There are some letters given to you below. This will help you solve the other words and unlock more characters. **Good Luck.**

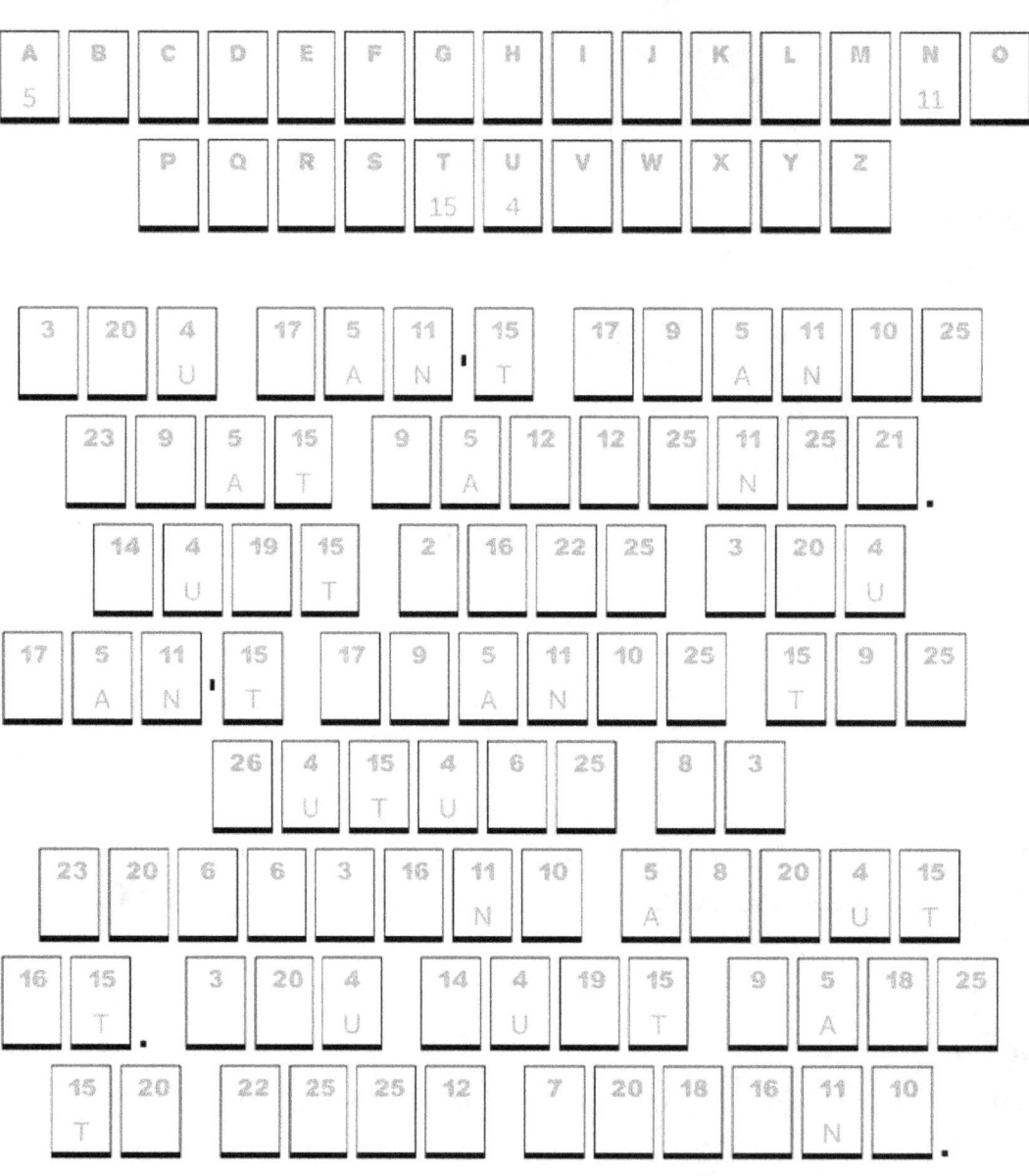

Wanda Sykes

Wanda Sykes

March 7, 1964 – PRESENT
COMEDIAN / ACTRESS

LEFT BLANK ON PURPOSE

Wanda Sykes

Wanda Sykes

Wanda Sykes

Wanda Sykes

Wanda Sykes

Wanda Sykes

Directions: read the bio below and answer the following questions.

Hi, my name is Wanda Yvette Sykes. I was born on March 7, 1964, in Portsmouth, VA. I graduated from Arundel High School. I got my Bachelor of Science degree in marketing from Hampton University. I became a member of the Alpha Kappa Alpha sorority. I started as a contracting specialist at the National Security Agency (NSA). I started my stand-up career at a Coors Light Super Talent Showcase in Washington, DC while I was still working at the NSA. In the 1990s, I appeared on Russell Simmons' Def Comedy Jam. After opening for Chris Rock at Caroline's Comedy Club I joined his writing team in 1997 for The Chris Rock Show. In 1997, I made my TV debut on The Chris Rock Show. In 1998, I made my film debut in the movie Tomorrow Night. Here are some more of the films and TV shows that I have participated in: The Drew Carey Show, Nutty Professor II: The Klumps, Curb Your Enthusiasm, Ice Age: Collision Course, The New Adventures of Old Christine and Breaking News in Yuba County.

1. What is the name of my sorority?
    A. Delta Gamma Theta
    B. Sigma Gamma Rho
    C. Alpha Kappa Alpha
2. What HBCU did I go to?
    A. Spellman College
    B. Hampton University
    C. Fisk University
3. What show did I get to write for and play a role in?
    A. The Keenen Ivory Wayans Show
    B. Will & Grace
    C. The Chris Rock Show

Directions: Answer the questions, to solve the crossword puzzle. You can use the internet if you get stuck on any question.

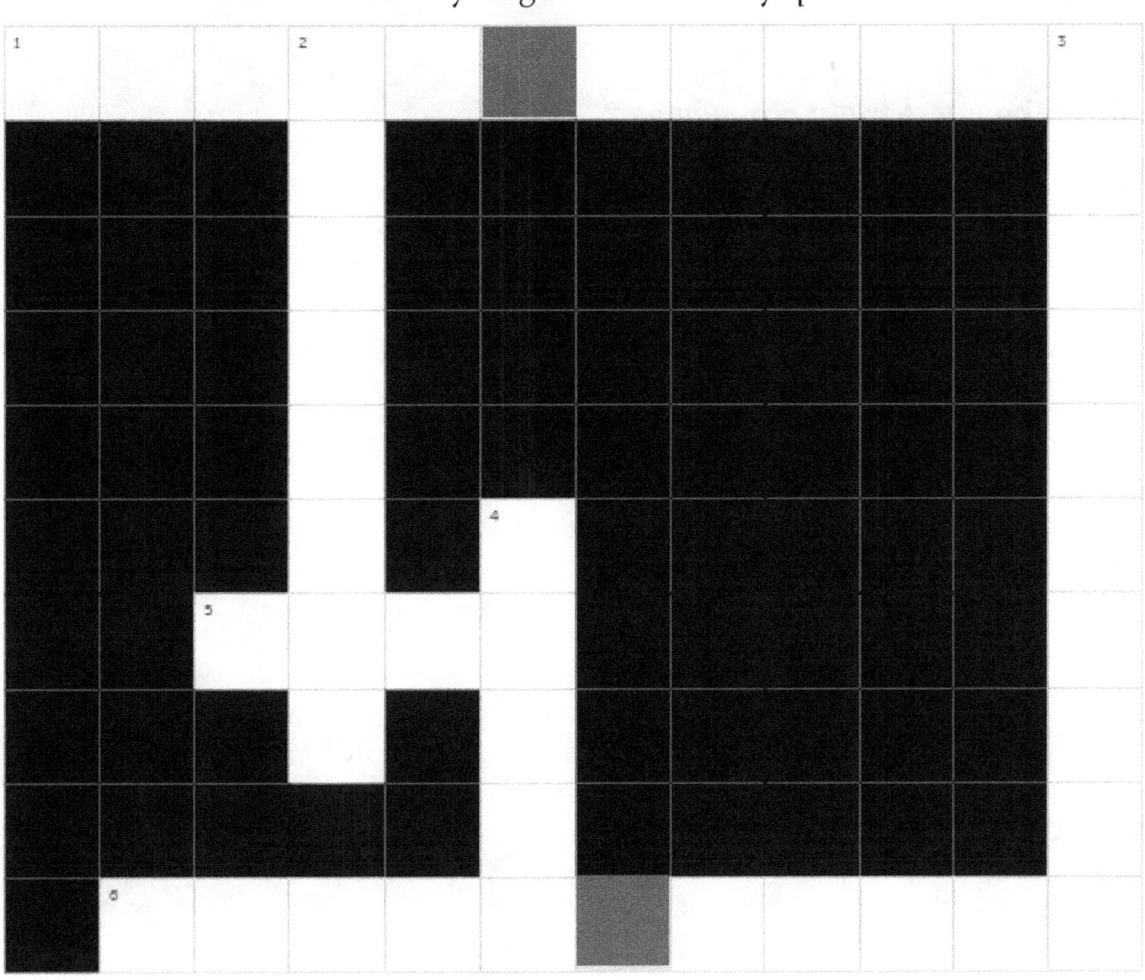

Across

1) Wanda won a GLAAD award for promoting a good image of ____ for gays and lesbians.
5) Wanda's first book was titled "____, I Said It."
6) Wanda performed for the first time in front of a live audience at a ____ Super Talent Showcase

Down

2) Wanda was heard in the ____ feature "Ice Age: Continental Drift" as 'Granny.'
3) Wanda first job was as a contracting ____ at the National Security Agency.
4) Wanda's first big break came when opening for ____ Rock.

Directions: read and answer the questions. These are your opinions so the answers will vary.

Could you be a late night comedy act?

What's your favorite Wanda Sykes movie?

Where do you hope to live someday?

Directions: unscramble the words below about Wanda. See if you can get the bonus word.

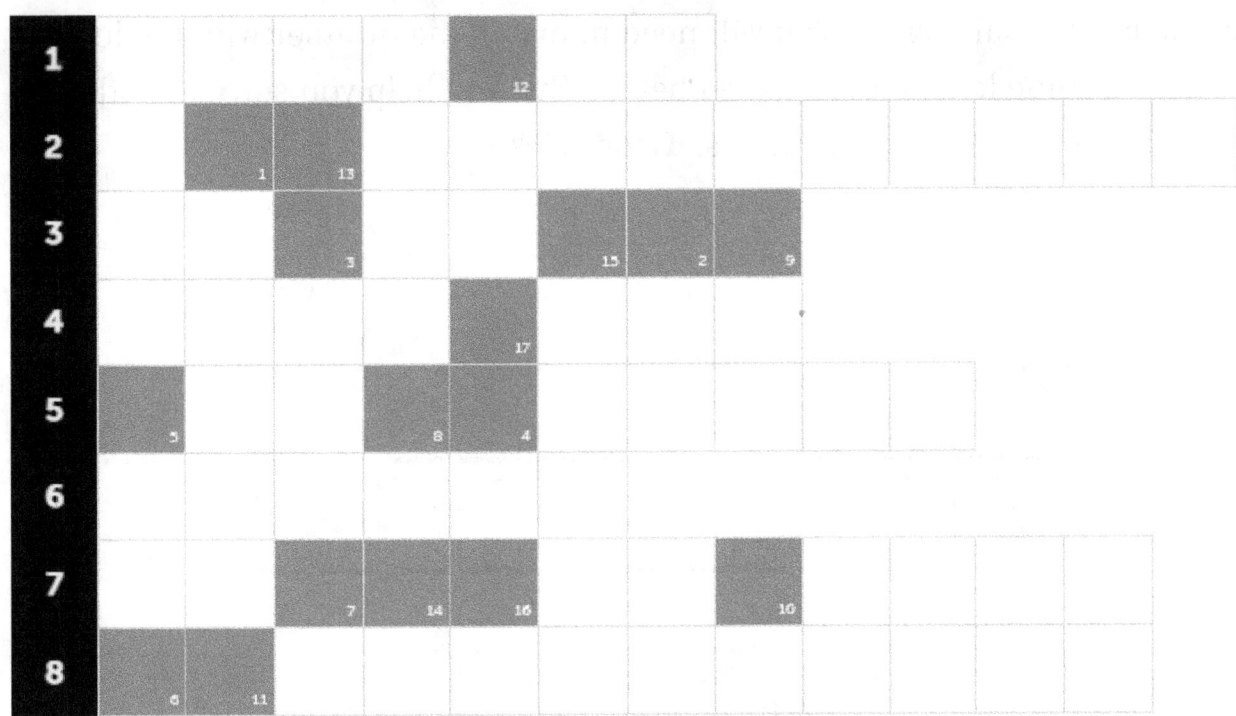

BONUS WORD

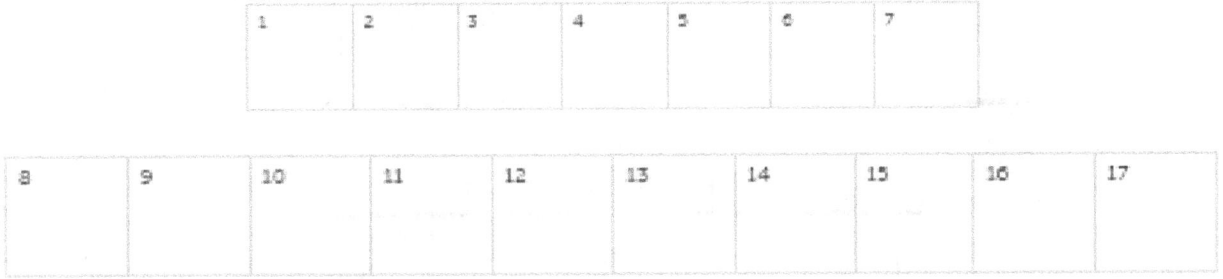

Unscramble Words

1) saretsc
2) osrscrikhcowh
3) conadiem
4) daryabnr
5) swuhaesthp
6) terirw
7) lorintswmean
8) ehgeohrvdeet

Directions: This is the WGLT Challenge. Solve the cryptogram. As the puzzle solver, you need to find which number belongs to which character. And this can be pretty challenging! You will need to match the number with the letter. There are some letters given to you below. This will help you solve the other words and unlock more characters. **Good Luck.**

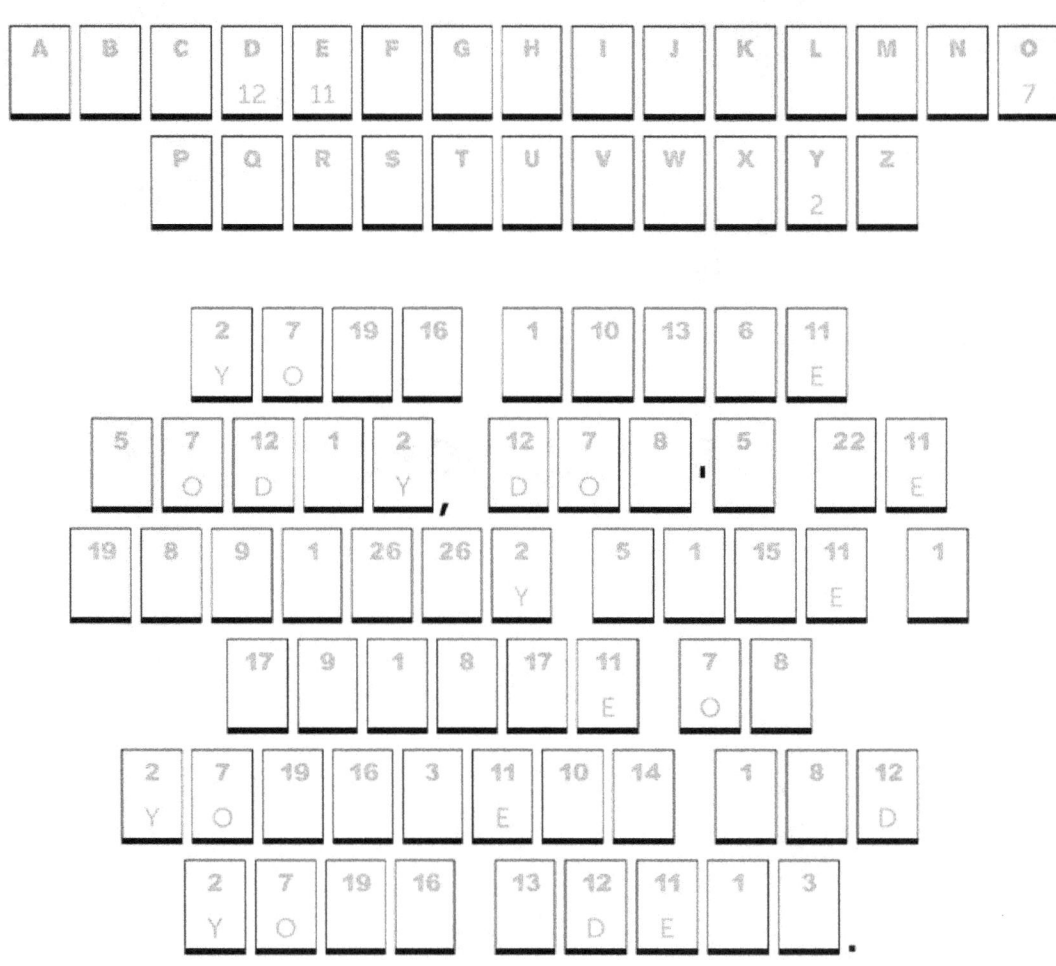

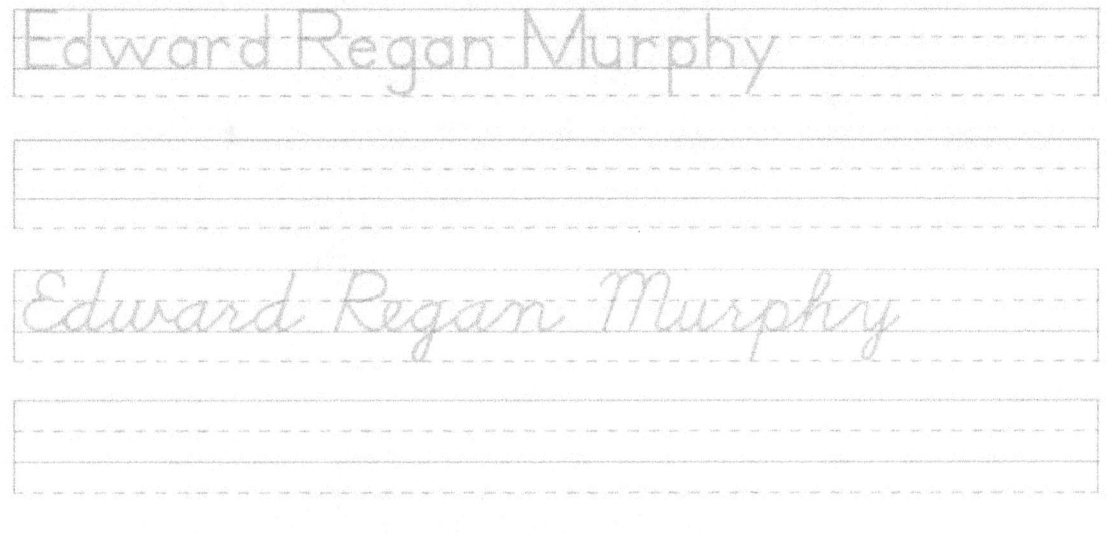

April 3, 1961 – PRESENT
ACTROR / COMEDIAN

27

Edward Regan Murphy

Edward Regan Murphy

Edward Regan Murphy

Edward Regan Murphy

Edward Regan Murphy

Edward Regan Murphy

Directions: read the bio below and answer the following questions.

Hi, my name is Edward Regan Murphy. I was born on April 3, 1961, in Brooklyn, NY. I started imitating different people and characters when I was young. I was influenced by one of Richard Pryor's albums when I was 15. I started acting at a youth talent show, where I performed "Let's Stay Together" while impersonating Al Greene. I graduated from Roosevelt Junior-Senior High School. Shortly after that, I made my TV debut in 1980 by landing a job on "Saturday Night Live (SNL)", I was 19 at the time. I was also the only cast member to host SNL while I was still a regular. In 1982, I made my big-screen debut in the film 48 Hrs. In 1983, I starred in the film Trading Places with Dan Aykroyd. In 1989, I made my director debut while working on the film Harlem Nights. In 1995, I made my producer debut with the film Vampire in Brooklyn. I helped write and produce and starred in the movie Life. Some more of the films and TV that I have been in include The Nutty Professor, The PJs, Norbit, Shrek the Halls, Coming to America, Dr. Dolittle, Dreamgirls and Dolemite is My Name.

1. Who did I imitate in my youth talent show?
   A. Richard Pryor
   B. Al Greene
   C. Redd Foxx
2. What year did I start working at SNL?
   A. 1984
   B. 1982
   C. 1980
3. Which movie did I star in help write and produce?
   A. Life
   B. Mulan
   C. Daddy Day Care

Directions: find the words associated with Eddie's life and career.

A	J	K	D	P	B	T	A	P	P	M	O	X	I	R	N	J	U
C	T	G	W	H	Y	K	P	N	M	T	S	W	J	B	E	K	R
T	M	R	I	J	D	W	Y	U	S	W	V	K	Z	C	R	J	O
O	O	V	G	P	R	H	L	T	I	Q	F	S	Z	P	X	P	M
R	W	X	T	K	V	T	A	N	L	P	Y	K	X	K	O	E
E	H	M	Y	G	D	J	B	Y	G	D	F	I	E	S	U	C	O
Y	I	R	R	I	T	I	H	P	E	Z	L	S	R	D	R	S	A
V	P	R	E	H	Y	X	V	R	R	W	C	I	H	V	R	L	F
W	G	O	C	T	N	C	I	O	H	W	O	R	S	O	M	L	O
F	E	R	U	M	I	C	V	F	G	B	M	X	F	X	Z	I	G
H	K	Y	D	J	P	R	B	E	M	L	E	Q	P	H	Q	H	D
R	U	K	O	K	J	T	W	S	Q	C	D	Y	X	L	D	Y	K
O	U	C	R	D	I	K	N	S	O	K	I	X	C	M	D	L	Y
J	R	U	P	S	T	G	L	O	Y	N	A	L	U	M	W	R	Y
K	Q	Y	F	Y	V	R	T	R	R	X	N	F	T	N	C	E	X
S	S	A	C	B	N	Q	O	K	S	F	R	M	C	D	L	V	T
R	U	Y	K	P	N	H	R	X	U	T	W	T	B	V	T	E	N
C	O	M	I	N	G	T	O	A	M	E	R	I	C	A	U	B	M

Find These Words

SINGER   SHREK
PRODUCER   MULAN
COMEDIAN   COMINGTOAMERICA
ACTOR   NUTTYPROFESSOR
WRITER   BEVERLYHILLSCOP

31

Directions: read and answer the questions. These are your opinions so the answers will vary.

Would you rather play video games or play outside?

_____

_____

What's your favorite Eddie Murphy cartoon movie?

_____

_____

Describe the most beautiful place you've ever been.

_____

_____

_____

_____

_____

Directions: read and answer the questions below. There are clues in the puzzle to help you. Try and solve the cryptic message.

Clue for cryptic message: Eddie did the voice for this character.

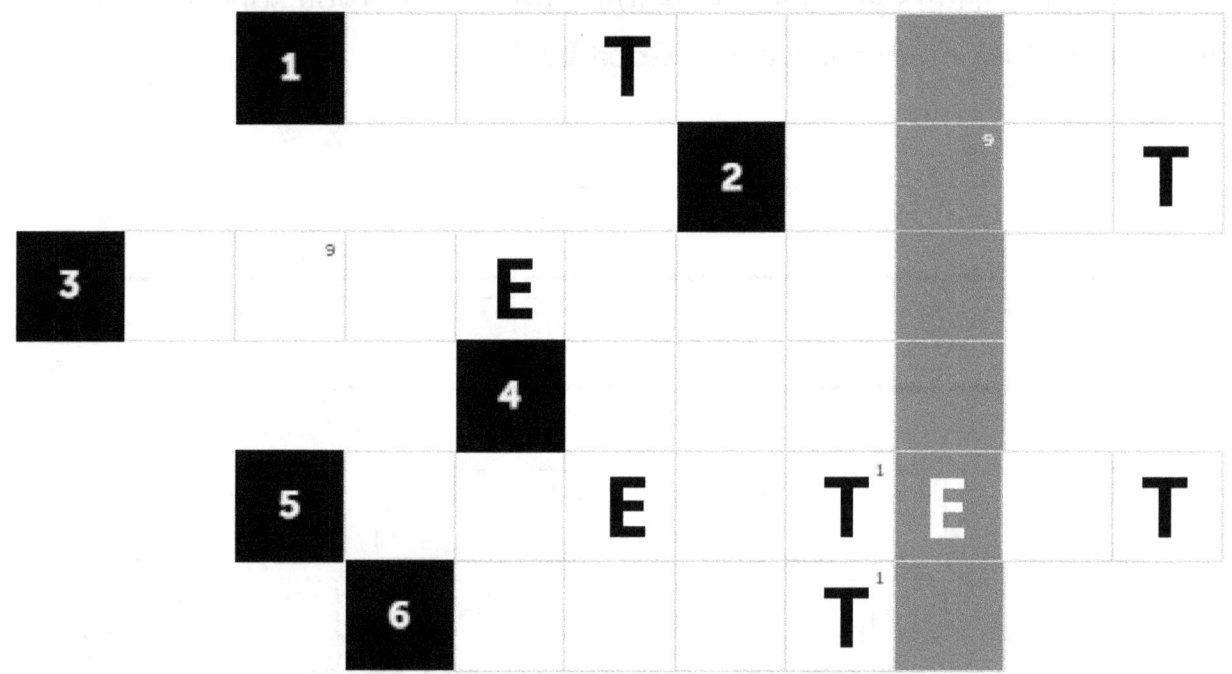

Questions

1) Eddie was a regular cast member on ____ Night Live for four years.

2) Eddie is the only Saturday Night Live cast member to ____ the show while still a regular.

3) Eddie's live album, "Eddie Murphy: ____" won a Grammy for Best Comedy Recording.

4) Eddie was awarded the ____ Twain Prize for American Humor.

5) Eddie is ranked No. 10 on Comedy Central's list of the 100 ____ Stand-ups of All Time as of 2022.

6) Eddie is also a singer and musician, with the hit single "____ All the Time".

Directions: This is the WGLT Challenge. Solve the cryptogram. As the puzzle solver, you need to find which number belongs to which character. And this can be pretty challenging! You will need to match the number with the letter. There are some letters given to you below. This will help you solve the other words and unlock more characters. **Good Luck.**

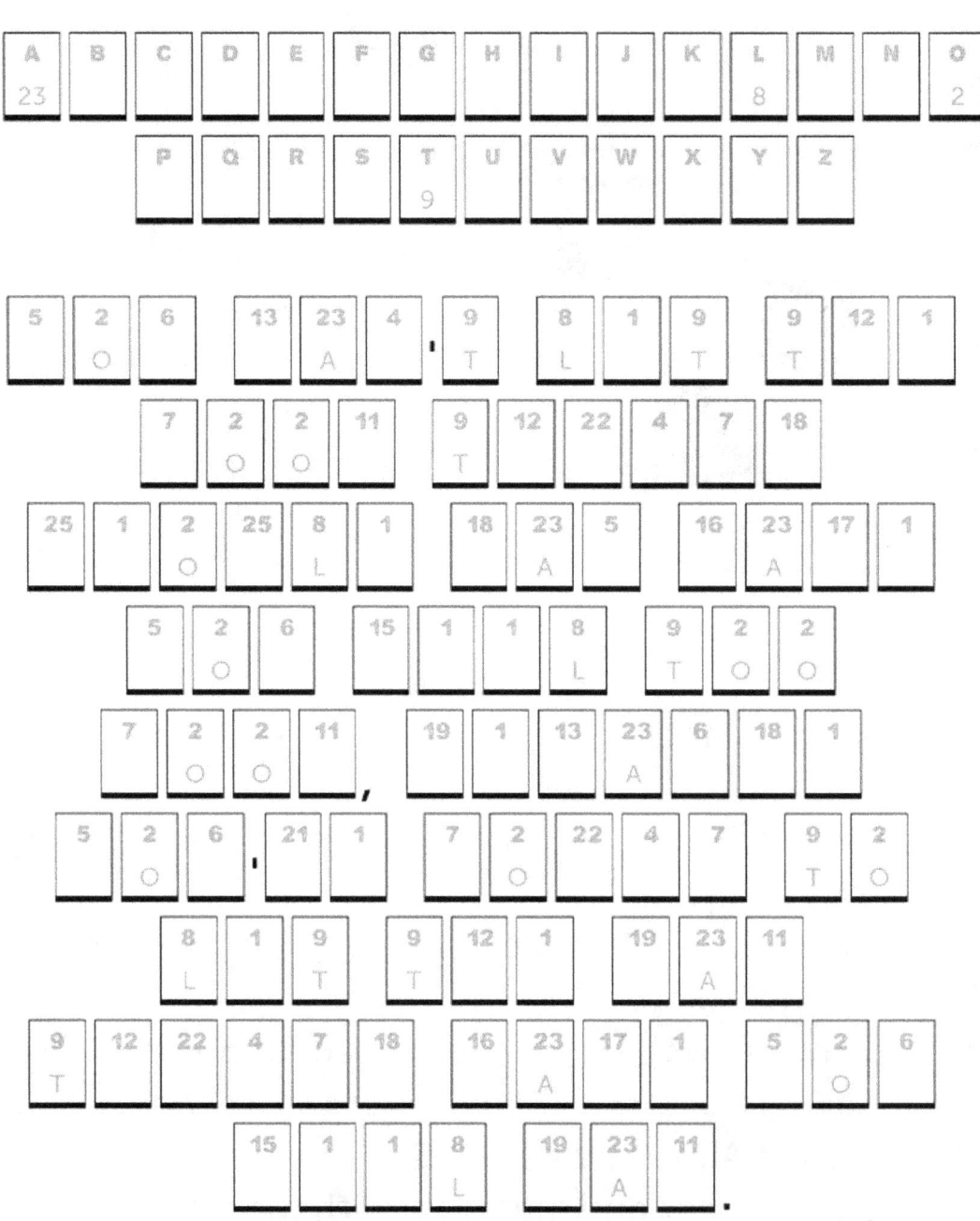

Caryn Elaine Johnson

Caryn Elaine Johnson

November 13, 1955 –PRESENT
ACTOR / COMEDIAN

LEFT BLANK ON PURPOSE

Caryn Elaine Johnson

Caryn Elaine Johnson

Caryn Elaine Johnson

Caryn Elaine Johnson

Caryn Elaine Johnson

Caryn Elaine Johnson

Directions: read the bio below and answer the following questions.

Hi, my name is Caryn Elaine Johnson. I was born on November 13, 1955, in Manhattan, NY. I attended Washington Irving High School. I got my stage forename ("Whoopi") from the phrase "whoopee cushion." People used to say to me, "You're like a whoopee cushion." That's where the name came from. In 1982, I made my film debut in Citizen: I'm Not Losing My Mind, I'm Giving It Away. In 1984, I made my Broadway debut with the show Whoopi Goldberg. In 1990, I became the second Black woman to win an Academy Award for acting in the film Ghost. In 1994, I became the first Black woman to host the Academy Awards ceremony. I achieved the EGOT after winning the four major American awards for professional entertainers: an Emmy (television), a Grammy (music), an Oscar (film) and a Tony (theater). I'm the first Black woman to have achieved all four awards. I'm the first African American actor to have received Academy Award nominations for both Best Actress and Best Supporting Actress.

1. Where did I get my stage name from?
    A. My Mom
    B. The phrase whoopee cushion
    C. My acting teacher
2. I'm the first black woman to have achieved what?
    A. To win Academy Award for Best Supporting Actress
    B. To achieve EGOT status
    C. To win Academy Award for Best Actress
3. I became the first black woman to host?
    A. The Academy Awards
    B. Good Morning America
    C. The Golden Globe Awards

Directions: answer the questions, to solve the crossword puzzle. You can use the internet if you get stuck on any question.

Across

1) Whoopi was in the film, "The _____". She received a Best Leading Actress Academy Award nomination.
4) Whoopi and her daughter Martin starred in ____ 2: Back in the Habit.
5) Whoopi performed all her own ___ numbers in Sister Act.
6) Whoopi was the first woman to host the ____ on her own.

Down

2) Whoopi played Oda Mae Brown the whacky ___ in the film, "Ghost".
3) Whoopi's inspiration to be an actress came from the original Uhura on ___.

Directions: read and answer the questions. These are your opinions so the answers will vary.

Would you like to perform on Broadway one day? Why or Why not?

What's your favorite activity to do at recess?

Share a special memory you had with a friend.

Directions: unscramble the words below about Whoopi. See if you can get the bonus word.

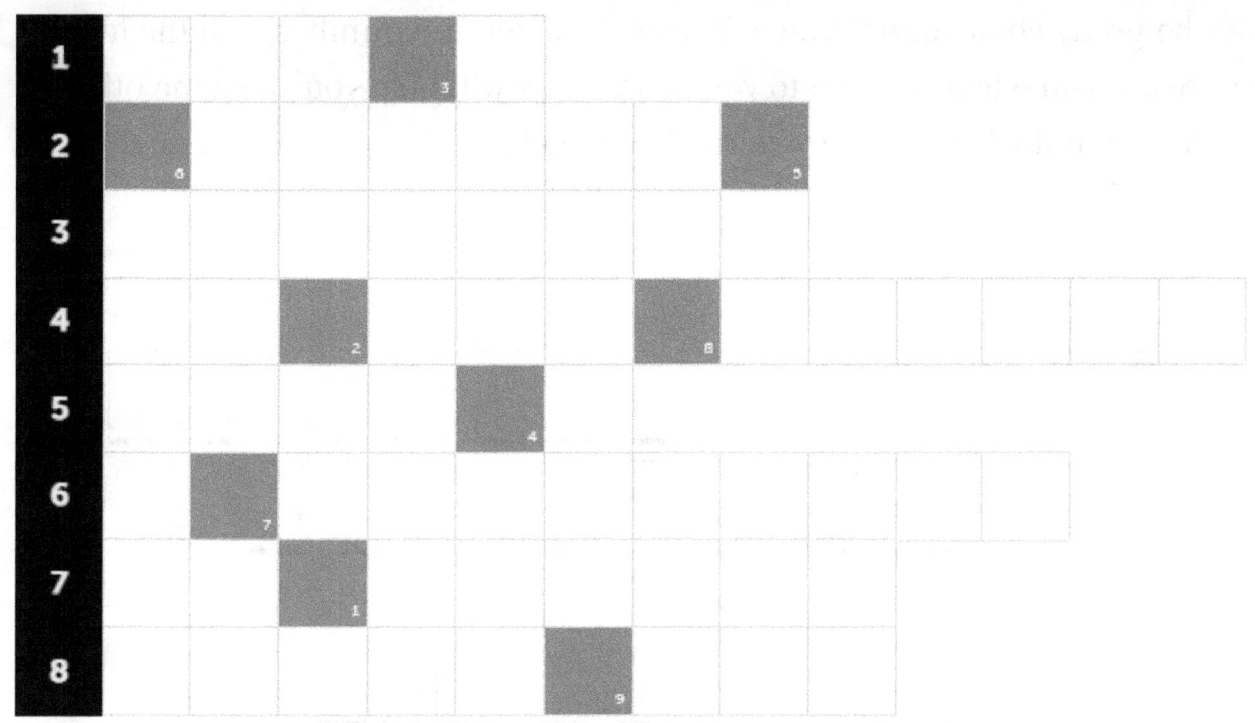

BONUS WORD

Unscramble Words

1) tocra
2) esarttkr
3) dioacnme
4) nipveatsytorl
5) arhuto
6) geihlnitnok
7) esriacstt
8) dayoarnwt

41

Directions: This is the WGLT Challenge. Solve the cryptogram. As the puzzle solver, you need to find which number belongs to which character. And this can be pretty challenging! You will need to match the number with the letter. There are some letters given to you below. This will help you solve the other words and unlock more characters. **Good Luck.**

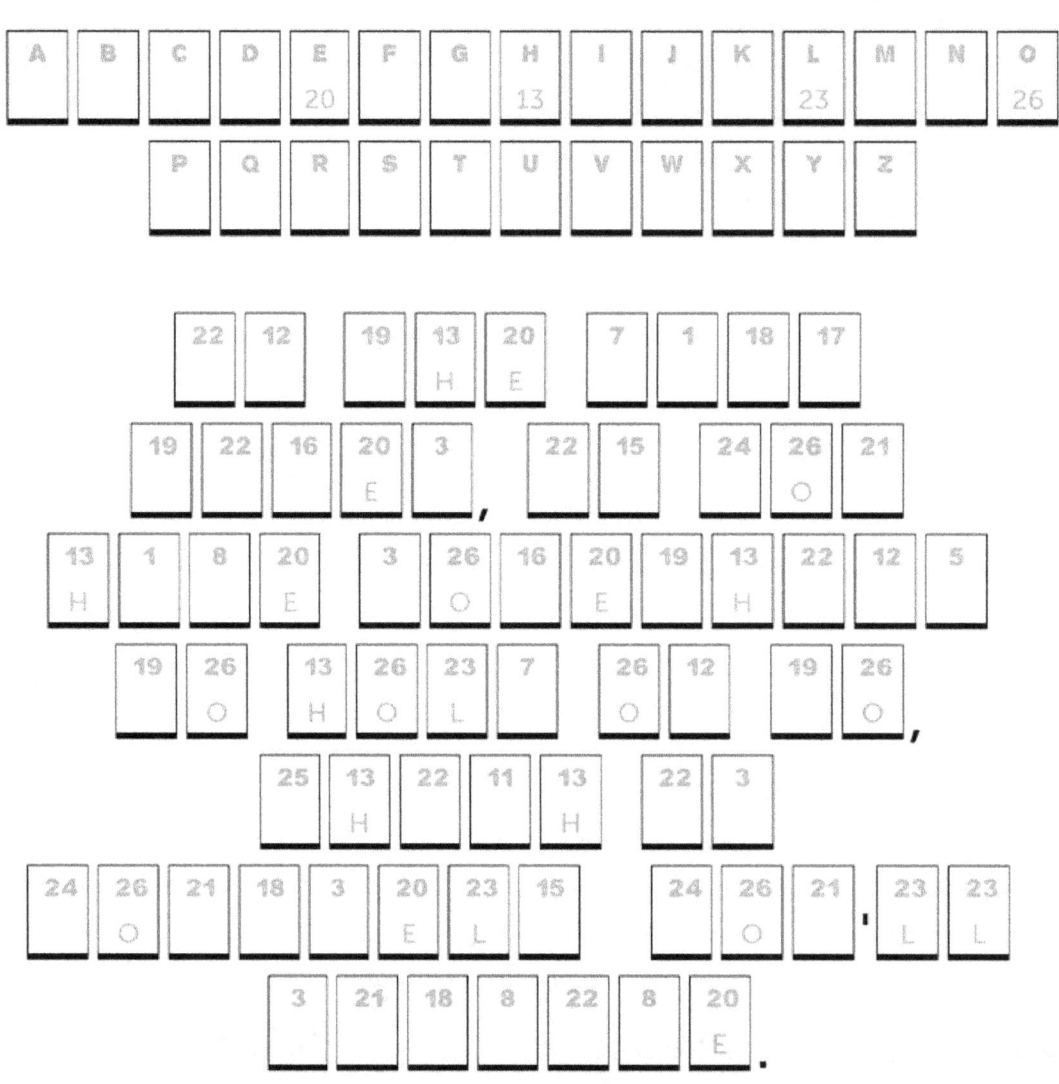

42

David Chappelle

David Chappelle

August 24, 1973 – PRESENT
COMEDIAN / ACTOR

43

LEFT BLANK ON PURPOSE

David Chappelle

David Chappelle

David Chappelle

David Chappelle

David Chappelle

David Chappelle

Directions: read the bio below and answer the following questions.

Hi, my name is David Khari Webber Chappelle. I was born on August 24, 1973, in Washington, D.C. I graduated from Duke Ellington School of the Arts. I started performing at Harlem's Apollo Theater and became part of the New York comedy circuit. I even performed in the city's parks. I did weekend stand-up gigs and "open mic" performances at the Boston Comedy Club. In 1992, I was on Russell Simmons' Def Comedy Jam on HBO. After that, I became a regular guest on late-night television shows such as Politically Incorrect, the Late Show with David Letterman, The Howard Stern Show and Late Night with Conan O'Brien. At 19, I made my film debut in Mel Brooks' Robin Hood: Men in Tights. I also appeared on Star Search three times. One year, I was the opening act for Aretha Franklin. In 1998, I co-wrote and starred in the film Half Baked. In 2000, I recorded my first hour-long HBO special, Dave Chappelle: Killin' Them Softly. In 2003, I debuted in my own weekly sketch comedy show on Comedy Central called Chappelle's Show.

1. What was the name of the High School I graduate from?
   A. Eastern High School
   B. Anacostia High School
   C. Duke Ellington School of the Arts
2. What show did I start getting film and tv recognition?
   A. Def Comedy Jam
   B. Star Search
   C. Apollo Theater
3. What show did I co-write and star in?
   A. The Nutty Professor
   B. Half Baked
   C. Undercover Brother

Directions: find the words associated with Dave's life and career.

```
N Z E U P M F V B M Q M B M N M Y Z
H N I N E N R O B S I R A T S A E Y
R T P D U C R H H G T O P H M C T F
S E T E M Y C R O O M B Q D H R H
Y A G R H E N N O C Y M J Q W A K K
U F S C A K Q Z T L S T F A X P V Q
S X I O L C D L C O U N Z R O P D D
P H K V F G Q W A S B Y C - W E I F
P O S E - Z L F T L R O Q I Q L K J
J M I R B Y M V M I M V M H W L J K
B C K B A T C Z F E E B S C B E W D
G Q E R K X P M D R H F I D O S O H
W I S O E J U I S M O P B W Q H I C
G T T T D C A J B T D L T E L O C F
R P Q H C N S E C W R I T E R W A B
Z T F E L R O H I O T I M B V S Q O
S Q J R W P A S I O E C S V G C X M
W E S O C V G R A M M Y A W A R D N
```

Find These Words

WRITER
ACTOR
COMEDIAN
ASTARISBORN
GRAMMYAWARD

HALF-BAKED
CHI-RAQ
UNDERCOVERBROTHER
OHIO
CHAPPELLESHOW

47

Directions: Read and answer the questions. These are your opinions so the answers will vary.

Would you rather do comedy or music and why?

What's your favorite book & why?

What are you most excited about doing when you are a teen then college student and then an adult?

Directions: read and answer the questions below. There are clues in the puzzle to help you. Try and solve the cryptic message.

Clue for cryptic message: Dave starred in this series.

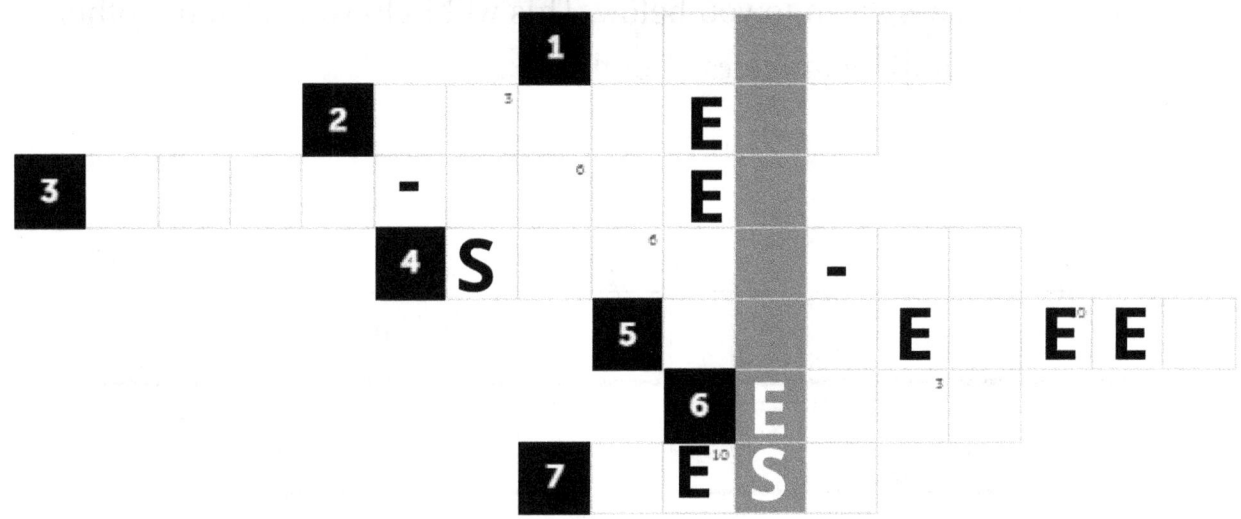

Questions

1) Dave's first film role was in "____ Hood: Men In Tights".
2) Dave performed at Harlem's famed Apollo Theater in front of the infamous "____ Night" audience, but he was booed off stage.
3) Dave's first lead role was in the 1998 comedy film ____, which he co-wrote with Neal Brennan.
4) Dave played a ___ insult comic who targets patrons of a nightclub in "The Nutty Professor".
5) Dave landed his first acting performance at the age of ____.
6) Dave got an ____ Award for appearing on the Saturday Night Live show.
7) Dave won a Grammy Award for ___ Comedy Album for his "Sticks and Stones" comedy album.

49

Directions: This is the WGLT Challenge. Solve the cryptogram. As the puzzle solver, you need to find which number belongs to which character. And this can be pretty challenging! You will need to match the number with the letter. There are some letters given to you below. This will help you solve the other words and unlock more characters. **Good Luck.**

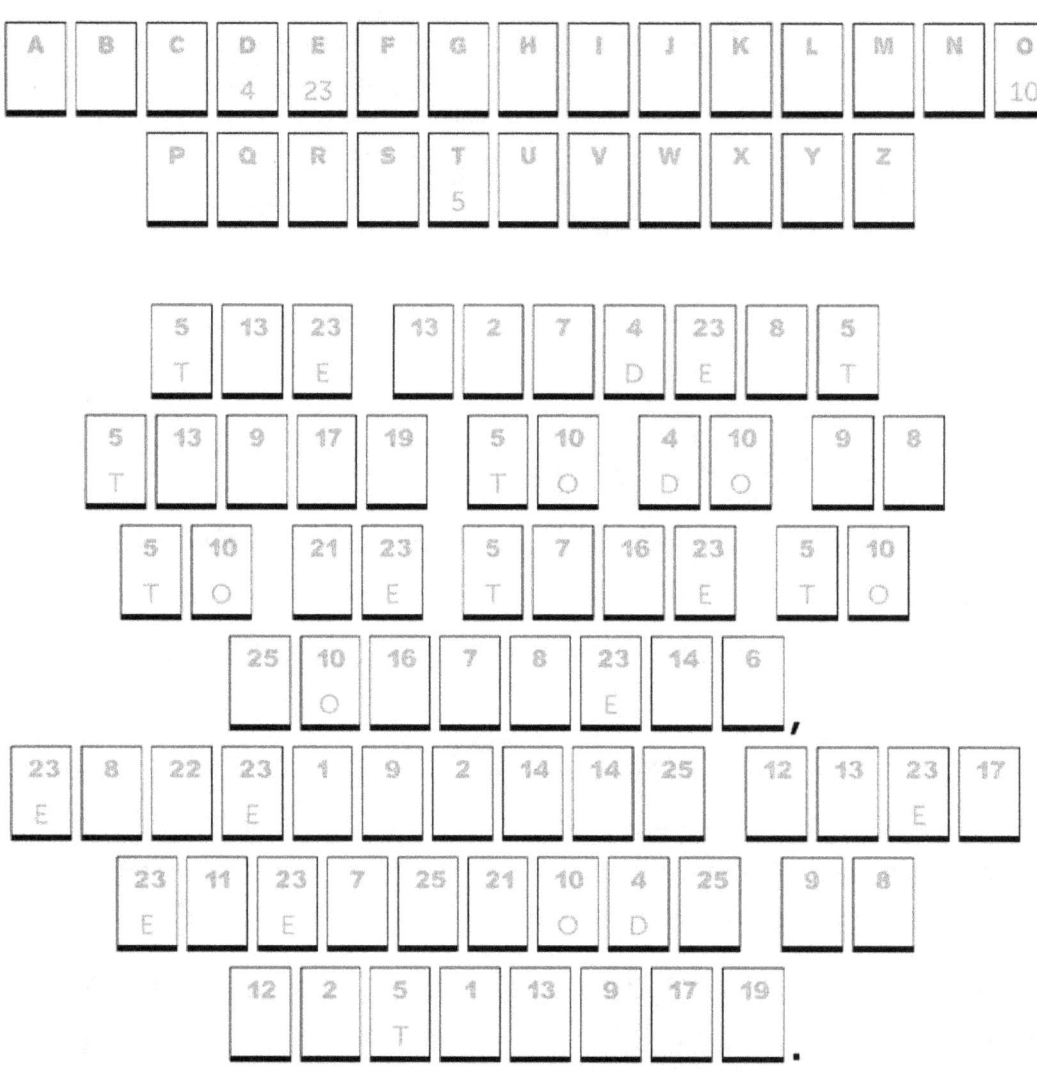

LaWanda Page

LaWanda Page

OCTOBER 19, 1920 – SEPTEMBER 14, 2002
ACTRESS / COMEDIAN

LEFT BLANK ON PURPOSE

LaWanda Page

LaWanda Page

LaWanda Page

LaWanda Page

LaWanda Page

LaWanda Page

Directions: read the bio below and answer the following questions.

Hi, my name is Alberta Peal. I was born on October 19, 1920, in Cleveland, OH. I started my career when I was 15 in St. Louis, where I learned how to fire-dance. I also learned to swallow fire, light matches and cigarettes with my fingertips and walk over flames. I was given the nicknames "The Bronze Goddess of Fire" and "LaWanda, the Flame Goddess" while performing at nightclubs. I used to perform on the Chitlin' Circuit and shared the stage with Redd Foxx and Richard Pryor at times. I joined the comedy act Skillet G Leroy. We became Skillet, Leroy G Company. During that time, I was called "The Queen of Comedy" and "The Black Queen of Comedy." I had a gold-selling album called Watch It, Sucker, which was based on my character Aunt Esther in Sanford and Son. In 1972, I made my TV debut when I got a call from my childhood friend Redd Foxx to appear in his NBC sitcom Sanford and Son. I auditioned and got the part of Aunt Esther, who became one of the iconic characters of the show.

1. What wasn't my nickname while I was fire dancing?
   A. The Bronze Goddess of Fire
   B. The Black Queen of Comedy
   C. LaWanda, the Flame Goddess
2. What year did I start working in TV?
   A. 1972
   B. 1971
   C. 1973
3. I'm best known as which character?
   A. The Bronze Goddess of Fire
   B. Aunt Esther
   C. The Black Queen of Comedy

Directions: answer the questions, to solve the crossword puzzle. You can use the internet if you get stuck on any question.

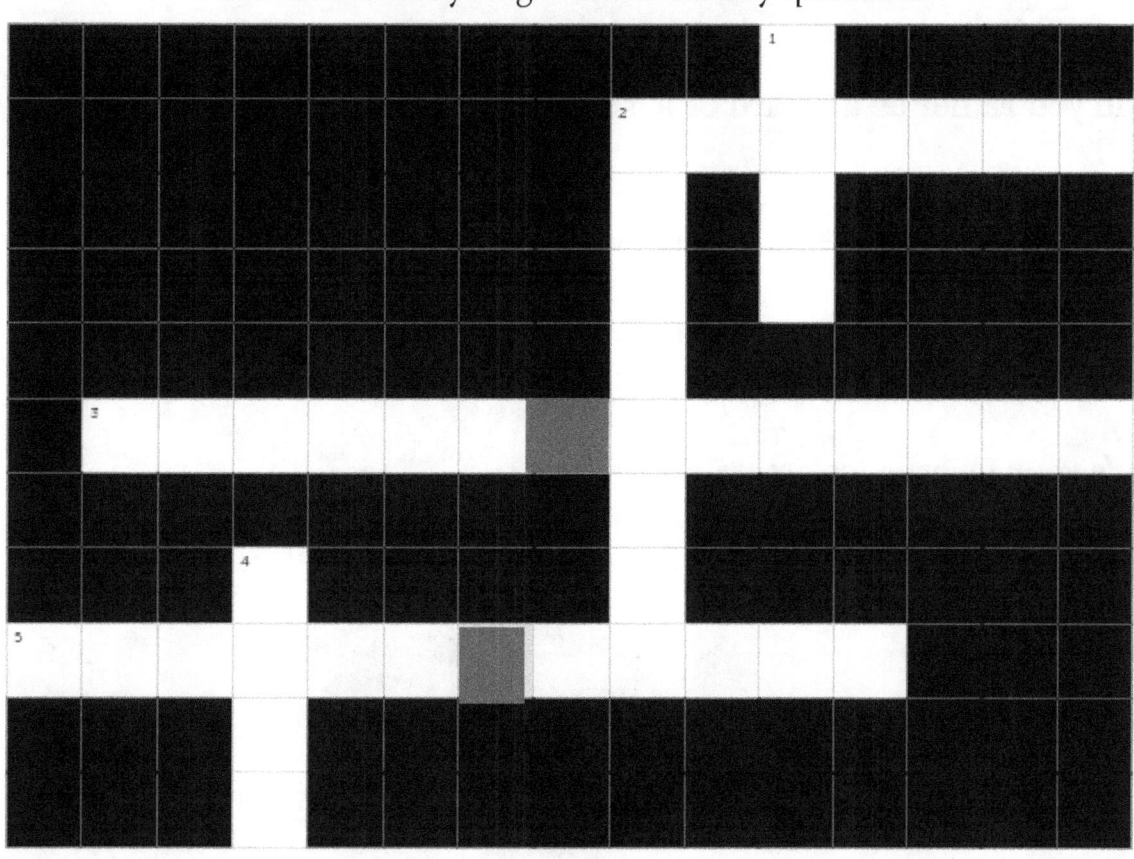

Across

2) LaWanda had recurring roles on several television series, one was '____ and Hutch'.

3) LaWanda use to dance with fire, swallow fire, lighting matches and cigarettes with her fingertips, known as "The ___ of Fire".

5) LaWanda's most popular live ___ 'Watch It, Sucker!' sold over 500,000 units.

Down

1) LaWanda released a number of live comedy albums under the label '___ Records.

2) LaWanda began working as a _____ at a nightclub called 'Collins Corner' when she was 15.

4) LaWanda's childhood friend ___ Foxx offered her a role in his hit show Sanford and Son as Aunt Esther.

Directions: read and answer the questions. These are your opinions so the answers will vary.

Would you rather be a wizard or a superhero?

What's your favorite ice cream flavor?

Share a time when you saw a show at the fair.

Directions: unscramble the words below about LaWanda. See if you can get the bonus word.

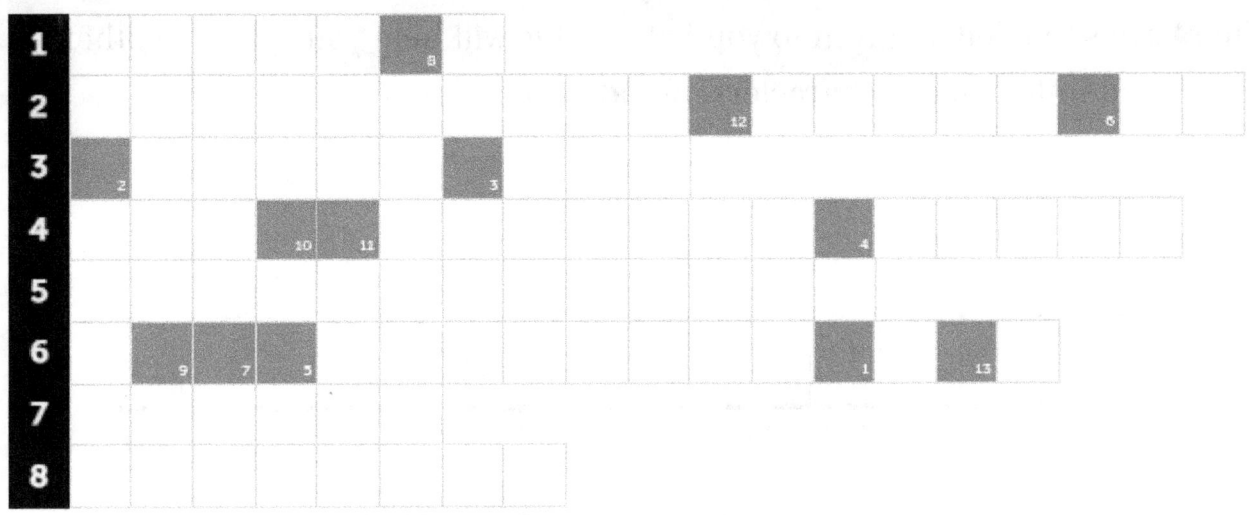

BONUS WORD

Unscramble Words

1) sescrta
2) nogrerebdofsfsieodz
3) rhtutnease
4) cncafldyemeebukoqo
5) ofaondadnrssn
6) ulhswtfaadiharmo
7) ydarif
8) ocedianm

57

Directions: This is the WGLT Challenge. Solve the cryptogram. As the puzzle solver, you need to find which number belongs to which character. And this can be pretty challenging! You will need to match the number with the letter. There are some letters given to you below. This will help you solve the other words and unlock more characters. **Good Luck.**

John Elroy Sanford

John Elroy Sanford

DECEMBER 9, 1922 – OCTOBER 11, 1991
COMEDIAN / ACTOR

LEFT BLANK ON PURPOSE

John Elroy Sanford

John Elroy Sanford

John Elroy Sanford

John Elroy Sanford

John Elroy Sanford

John Elroy Sanford

Directions: read the bio below and answer the following questions.

Hi, my name is John Elroy Sanford. I was born on December 9, 1922, in St. Louis, MO. I always had a reddish complexion and red hair, so I was given the nickname "Redd." I got "Foxx" from the baseball player Jimmie Foxx, whom I admired. I moved to Chicago at an early age and received the nickname "Chicago Red." I use to work with a man by the name of "Detroit Red," whom you may know now as "Malcolm X." I began performing as a comedian and actor in Black theaters and nightclubs on the Chitlin Circuit. In 1951, I worked with a friend of mine by the name of Slappy White. I was signed to a long-term contract with Dootone Records and I released a series of comedy albums. In 1972, my series Sanford and Son premiered on the NBC TV network. I was able to bring a few fellow comedians with me on this journey. The most famous was LaWanda Page, who played Aunt Esther. In 1960, I made my film debut in All the Fine Young Cannibals. In 1977, I had my own show, The Redd Foxx Comedy Hour. In 1989, I played Bennie Wilson in Harlem Nights.

1. Who inspired me for my stage name?
    A. Chad Fox
    B. Jake Fox
    C. Jimmie Foxx
2. What year did I start acting in film?
    A. 1960
    B. 1955
    C. 1965
3. What was the name of my first show on TV?
    A. The Redd Foxx Comedy Hour
    B. Sandford and Son
    C. Sandford

62

Directions: find the words associated with John's life and career.

M	K	X	B	T	F	J	B	J	A	G	T	N	Z	N	O	B	P
T	R	C	V	D	K	Z	S	I	U	O	L	.	T	S	T	S	D
H	D	Q	U	Q	K	R	B	W	H	K	F	R	L	U	D	R	P
S	A	N	F	O	R	D	A	N	D	S	O	N	G	K	S	J	I
T	G	A	N	T	Y	E	R	C	X	F	N	P	Y	U	G	E	R
R	S	W	P	Y	L	I	M	A	F	L	A	Y	O	R	E	H	T
G	O	L	D	E	N	G	L	O	B	E	A	W	A	R	D	W	S
H	A	R	L	E	M	N	I	G	H	T	S	N	Q	O	S	S
N	X	H	V	S	Y	G	F	W	F	T	N	F	W	H	G	R	A
Z	P	T	L	R	V	E	I	H	S	A	M	L	S	A	U	B	G
L	C	Y	O	I	L	M	B	H	I	W	R	X	G	N	D	T	E
D	F	T	J	B	X	Z	G	D	S	L	X	G	T	V	I	F	V
B	C	P	C	E	O	B	E	C	G	O	N	A	I	J	W	V	S
A	Y	P	B	F	R	M	J	P	F	I	F	R	X	Z	H	U	A
M	J	B	J	D	O	X	E	D	N	W	X	V	C	M	L	L	L
A	X	B	E	C	O	S	D	N	R	V	J	B	H	X	T	S	B
O	J	O	Q	K	N	E	U	Y	S	B	L	Q	Q	S	Y	T	G
I	F	L	I	V	R	R	X	E	M	P	R	V	Z	E	A	G	E

Find These Words

COMEDIAN	THEROYALFAMILY
ACTOR	HARLEMNIGHTS
REDDFOXXSHOW	GOLDENGLOBEAWARD
ST.LOUIS	LASVEGASSTRIP
RUNNINGGAGS	SANFORDANDSON

63

Directions: read and answer the questions. These are your opinions so the answers will vary.

Would you rather work in a group or work alone?

What's your favorite hobby or after school activity?

Where do you want to go to college?

Directions: read and answer the questions below. There are clues in the puzzle to help you. Try and solve the cryptic message.

Clue for cryptic message: John did this at the begining of his career.

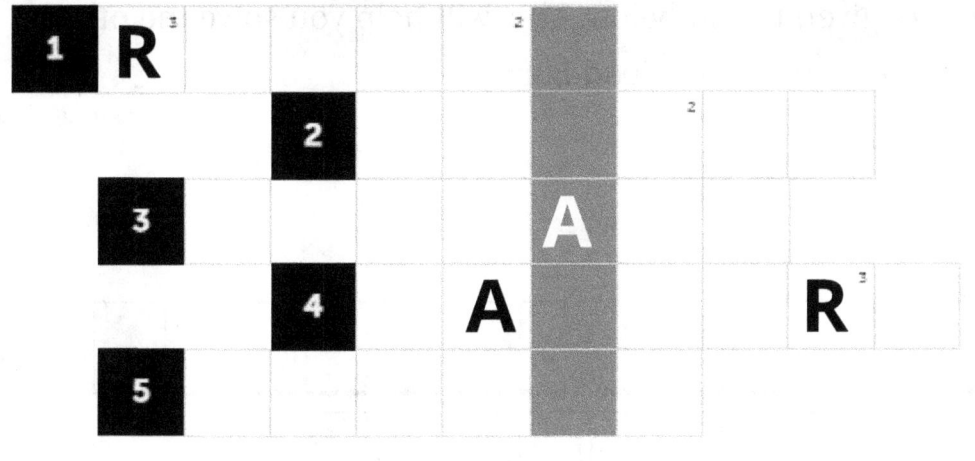

Questions

1) John was friends with the civil ___ leader Malcolm X.
2) John's co-star Cleavon Little in ___ Comes to Harlem suggested him for the role in Sanford and Son.
3) John's nickname was "___ Red" because of his hair color.
4) John was only forty-nine years old when he played the part of Fred ___.
5) John is ranked 24th in ___ Central Presents: 100 Greatest Stand-ups of All Time.
6) John was one of the first black comics to play to white ___ on the Las Vegas Strip.
7) John was known as the "King of the ___ Records", he performed on more than 50 records in his lifetime.

Directions: This is the WGLT Challenge. Solve the cryptogram. As the puzzle solver, you need to find which number belongs to which character. And this can be pretty challenging! You will need to match the number with the letter. There are some letters given to you below. This will help you solve the other words and unlock more characters. **Good Luck.**

Sheryl Underwood

Sheryl Underwood

October 28, 1963 – PRESENT
COMEDIAN / TV HOST

67

LEFT BLANK ON PURPOSE

Sheryl Underwood

Sheryl Underwood

Sheryl Underwood

Sheryl Underwood

Sheryl Underwood

Sheryl Underwood

Directions: read the bio below and answer the following questions.

Hi, my name is Sheryl Patrice Underwood. I was born on October 28, 1963, in Little Rock, AR. I graduated from Atwater High School. I got a Bachelor of Arts degree from the University of Chicago in Illinois and a master's degree from Governor's State University. I am also a member of the Zeta Phi Beta sorority. In 1981, I enlisted in the Air Force. I was a part of the O'Hare Air Reserve Station. In 1989, I was the first female finalist in the Miller Lite Comedy Search. In 1994, I won the BET "Funniest Female Comedian on ComicView" award. In 1998, I made my film debut in the movie Bulworth. In 2008, I was elected as the Grand Basileus of Zeta Phi Beta, which made me the first professional entertainer to hold the highest elected office in a National Pan-Hellenic Council organization. I am the founder of the Pack Rat Foundation for Education, which is a non-profit organization that raised money to support the 105 historically Black colleges and universities and students committed to pursuing higher education.

1. What was the name of college I got my degree from?
   A. Governor's State University
   B. Fresno City College
   C. University of Chicago
2. What sorority do I belong to?
   A. Alpha Kappa Alpha
   B. Zeta Phi Beta
   C. Delta Sigma Theta
3. I won what award from BET?
   A. Funniest Female Comedian on ComicView
   B. Best Actress
   C. Best Supporting Actress

Directions: answer the questions, to solve the crossword puzzle. You can use the internet if you get stuck on any question.

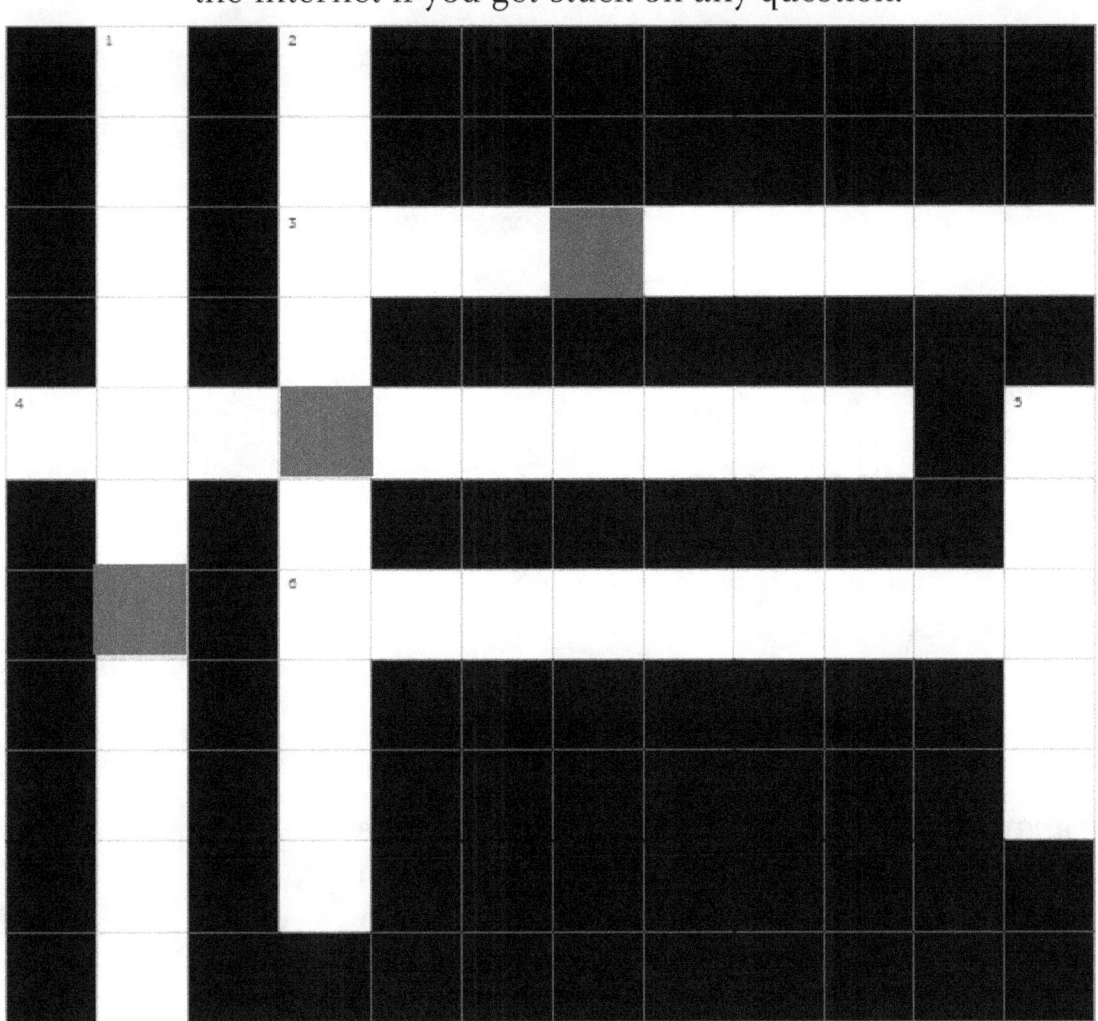

Across

3) Sheryl severed in the U.S _____ for a couple years.

4) Sheryl was a frequent performer in the 'HBO' comedy series '____ Jam.'

6) Sheryl made her acting debut with a small role in the ___ satire 'Bulworth.'

Down

1) Sheryl was the first female finalist in the _____ Comedy Search.

2) Sheryl played a recurring role in the _____, 'The Bold and the Beautiful.'

5) Sheryl produced and hosted a show titled '___.'

Directions: read and answer the questions. These are your opinions so the answers will vary.

What branch of the military do you like best?

What's your favorite meal of the day?

Share about a time you learned an important life lesson.

Directions: unscramble the words below about Sheryl. See if you can get the bonus word.

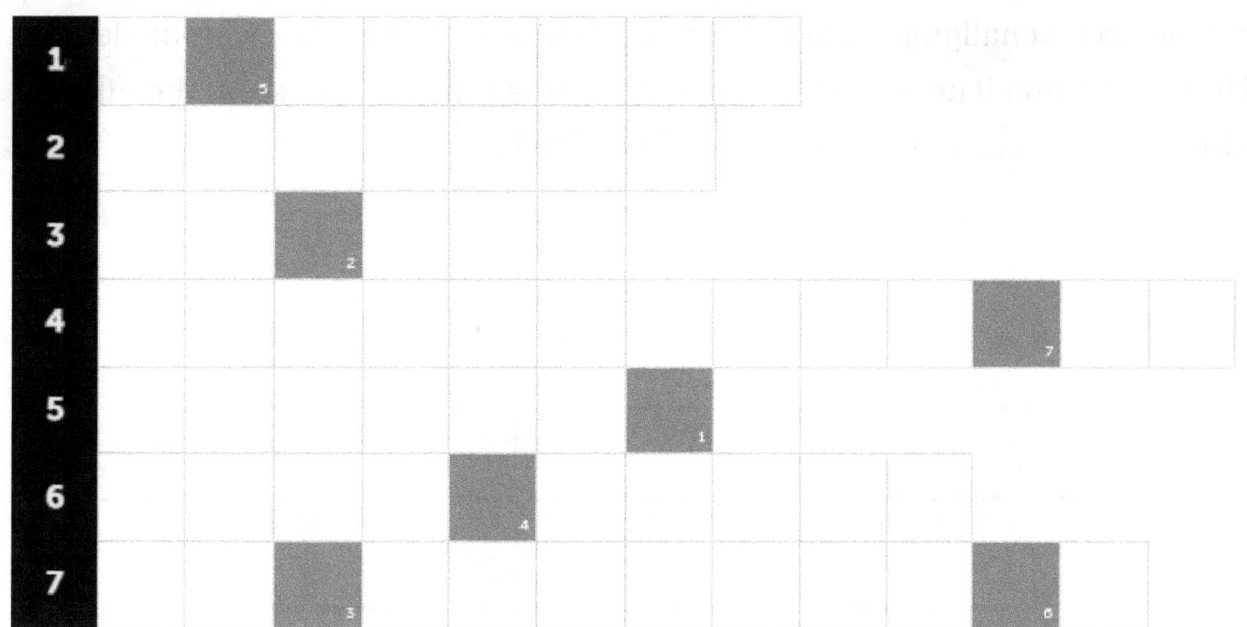

BONUS WORD

Unscramble Words

1) aioodern   **2)** sctsera   **3)** sovtth
4) uotihohoketpg   **5)** bortuhlw   **6)** thsoabpyue
7) hcoledputoed

Directions: This is the WGLT Challenge. Solve the cryptogram. As the puzzle solver, you need to find which number belongs to which character. And this can be pretty challenging! You will need to match the number with the letter. There are some letters given to you below. This will help you solve the other words and unlock more characters. **Good Luck.**

OCTOBER 12, 1932 – AUGUST 19, 2017
COMEDIAN / CIVIL RIGHTS LEADER

LEFT BLANK ON PURPOSE

Richard Claxton Gregory

Richard Claxton Gregory

Richard Claxton Gregory

Richard Claxton Gregory

Richard Claxton Gregory

Richard Claxton Gregory

Directions: read the bio below and answer the following questions.

Hi, my name is Richard Claxton Gregory. I was born on October 12, 1932, in St. Louis, MO. I graduated from Sumner High School. I attended Southern Illinois University but left early because I was drafted into the U.S. Army in 1954. I started performing stand-up comedy at this time. In 1961, I made my New York debut at The Blue Angel nightclub. That same year, I returned to Chicago, IL to work at the Playboy Club. I had one show that ran for six weeks and I got a spot in Time magazine. In 1963, I went to Selma, Alabama and spoke for two hours on a public platform two days before the voter registration drive known as "Freedom Day." In 1968, I ran for President of the United States as a write-in candidate of the Freedom and Peace Party. In 1979, I appeared at the Amandla Festival where Bob Marley, Patti LaBelle and Eddie Palmieri, among many others performed for the international Anti-Apartheid Movement. My monologues reflect a time when entertainment needed to be political to be relevant.

1. What was the branch of service that I served in?
   A. Navy
   B. Army
   C. Marine Corps
2. What year did I start doing comedy?
   A. 1954
   B. 1961
   C. 1958
3. I once ran for what branch of the U.S. government?
   A. Legislative
   B. Judicial
   C. Executive

Directions: find the words associated with Richard's life and career.

E	N	X	T	M	V	I	E	T	N	A	M	W	A	R	R	Y	L
H	I	U	V	D	G	P	W	E	B	J	T	L	X	P	M	P	S
H	K	M	Q	I	D	L	E	I	F	D	N	A	K	C	A	R	T
P	K	Y	C	D	N	G	E	Q	J	V	V	G	Q	D	Y	O	K
H	C	M	X	M	J	U	Y	H	X	O	I	C	W	M	O	S	I
O	K	B	I	K	P	E	R	Z	H	Z	O	P	X	D	R	R	Q
V	E	G	E	T	A	R	I	A	N	A	C	T	I	V	I	S	T
P	U	C	L	K	D	Z	C	H	H	U	P	V	S	P	S	M	I
I	U	S	A	R	M	Y	V	I	G	I	S	Y	H	C	G	C	O
H	H	S	V	T	T	H	E	B	L	U	E	A	N	G	E	L	Q
E	Y	F	X	U	T	Q	G	F	S	M	I	U	L	B	P	R	U
C	I	V	I	L	R	I	G	H	T	S	L	E	A	D	E	R	P
I	S	O	P	E	O	Q	L	J	I	I	G	D	A	U	H	E	F
A	K	M	E	A	R	G	Z	Q	A	C	L	G	P	D	G	K	P
V	C	I	O	R	W	Y	U	J	X	A	Q	J	P	M	U	C	Z
C	Q	F	T	G	Z	A	Y	Z	B	R	R	C	K	R	N	I	J
D	J	N	O	N	A	I	D	E	M	O	C	R	V	F	F	A	K
M	O	D	L	M	Q	V	A	L	S	T	A	N	D	U	P	G	J

Find These Words

COMEDIAN

CIVILRIGHTSLEADER

VEGETARIANACTIVIST

VIETNAMWAR

USARMY

MAYOR

RACISM

TRACKANDFIELD

THEBLUEANGEL

STANDUP

79

Directions: read and answer the questions. These are your opinions so the answers will vary.

Would you rather run for President or Governor?

What's your favorite board or card game?

What do you think you might be doing in 10 years?

Directions: read and answer the questions below. There are clues in the puzzle to help you. Try and solve the cryptic message.

Clue for cryptic message: Richard made fun of this in his acts.

Questions

1) Richard was drafted into the United States ___.
2) Richard ran for ___ of Chicago and president of the United States.
3) Richard was the first black performer to sit on the ___ of The Tonight Show.
4) Richard was an activist and a frontline figure in the civil ___ movement.
5) Richard received a track ___ to Southern Illinois University.
6) Richard got his start in ___ in the Army, where he entered and won several talent shows.

Directions: This is the WGLT Challenge. Solve the cryptogram. As the puzzle solver, you need to find which number belongs to which character. And this can be pretty challenging! You will need to match the number with the letter. There are some letters given to you below. This will help you solve the other words and unlock more characters. **Good Luck.**

February 6, 1957 – PRESENT
COMEDIAN / DIRECTOR

83

LEFT BLANK ON PURPOSE

Robert Townsend

Robert Townsend

Robert Townsend

Robert Townsend

Robert Townsend

Robert Townsend

Directions: read the bio below and answer the following questions.

Hi, my name is Robert Townsend. I was born on February 6, 1957, in Chicago, IL. I graduated from Austin High School. I began my acting career by joining The Experimental Black Actors Guild. In 1975, I made my film debut as an extra in the film Cooley High. In 1982, I appeared as one of the main characters in the PBS series Another Page. Some of the movies that I acted in include A Soldier's Story, The Mighty Quinn, American Flyers and Odd Jobs. In 1987, I wrote, directed, produced and starred in my first film, Hollywood Shuffle. It was a big success. In 1987, I directed Eddie Murphy: Raw. In 1991, I wrote, directed, produced and starred in what was probably my biggest film, The Five Heartbeats. I went on to direct many more movies after that, such as Little Richard, Carmen: A Hip Hopera, The Meteor Man, The Natalie Cole Story, Black Lightning, American Soul and The Wonder Years.

1. What was the name of my High School?
   A. Charles Evans Hughes High School
   B. Austin High School
   C. Morris High School
2. What year did I start acting?
   A. 1982
   B. 1975
   C. 1978
3. Which film did I Direct but not star in?
   A. Hollywood Shuffle
   B. The Five Heartbeats
   C. Black Lightning

Directions: answer the questions, to solve the crossword puzzle. You can use the internet if you get stuck on any question.

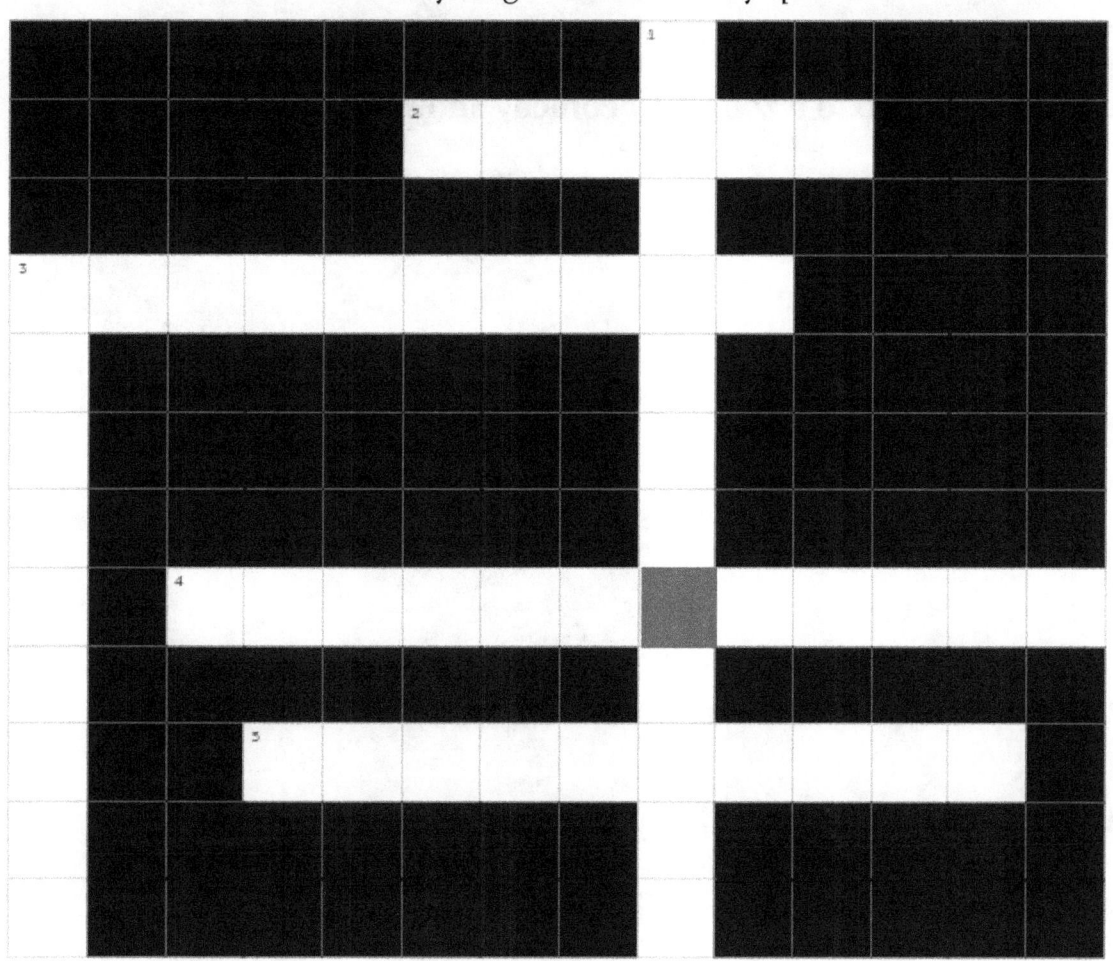

Across

2) Robert gained national exposure through his stand-up comedy routines and appearances on The Tonight Show Starring _____ Carson.
3) Robert wrote, directed and produced The Five _____.
4) Robert was in the film The _____ with Denzel Washington.
5) Robert created The Robert Townsend Foundation, a nonprofit organization whose mission is to introduce and help new unsigned _____.

Down

1) Robert was one of the main characters in the PBS series _____.
3) Robert wrote, directed and produced _____ Shuffle.

Directions: read and answer the questions. These are your opinions so the answers will vary.

Would you rather go to a zoo or an comedy show?

What's your favorite superhero?

Describe the most amazing thing you've ever seen in real life.

Directions: unscramble the words below about Robert. See if you can get the bonus word.

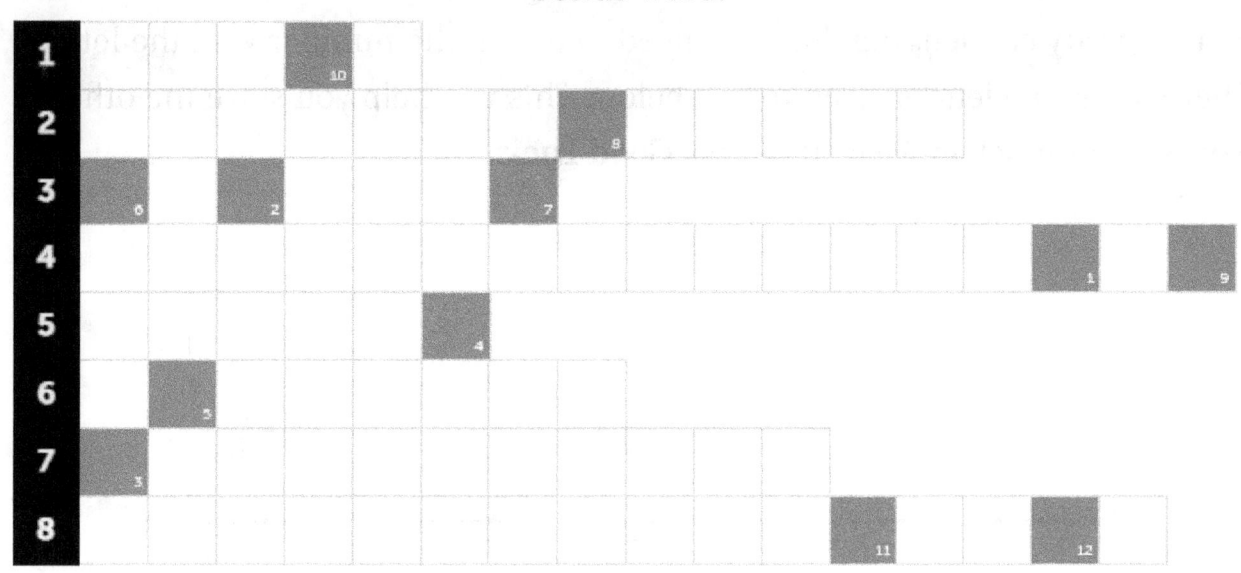

BONUS WORD

Unscramble Words

1) rcoat
2) oenparthdhteo
3) aoemcnid
4) tfhireeaevtebtsha
5) rretwi
6) dtieorrc
7) deeiymrdphu
8) lsooudfehlfhowly

89

Directions: This is the WGLT Challenge. Solve the cryptogram. As the puzzle solver, you need to find which number belongs to which character. And this can be pretty challenging! You will need to match the number with the letter. There are some letters given to you below. This will help you solve the other words and unlock more characters. **Good Luck.**

Lori Ann Rambough

Lori Ann Rambough

May 15, 1966 – PRESENT
COMEDIAN / ACTRESS

LEFT BLANK ON PURPOSE

Lori Ann Rambough

Lori Ann Rambough

Lori Ann Rambough

Lori Ann Rambough

Lori Ann Rambough

Lori Ann Rambough

Directions: read the bio below and answer the following questions.

Hi, my name is Lori Ann Rambough. I was born on May 15, 1966, in Trenton, NJ. I graduated from McCorristin Catholic High School (which is now called Trenton Catholic Academy). I got my bachelor's degree from Morris Brown College. In 1995, I made my TV debut in the show Snaps. Later that year, I performed on Def Comedy Jam. I hosted ComicView from 1995–1996. In 2001, I made my film debut in The Queens of Comedy and I was registered in The Guinness Book of World Records when I performed for a captivated audience of more than 50,000 people. Some of the films that I acted in are Friday After Next, It's Showtime at the Apollo, Soul Plane, The Parkers, Dirty Laundry, The Funniest Man Dead or Alive, A Miami Tail, Why We Laugh: Black Comedians on Black Comedy, South Side and The History of Comedy.

1. What was the name of the HBCU I went to?
    A. Spellman College
    B. Morris Brown College
    C. Howard University
2. What year did I debut in TV?
    A. 1995
    B. 1996
    C. 1994
3. I set what Guinness Book of World Records?
    A. Performing for more than 75,000 people
    B. Performing for more than 50,000 people
    C. Performing for more than 60,000 people

Directions: find the words associated with Lori's life and career.

```
Y M R S O U L P L A N E W P I N D V
J F N M K T D O S B L R Q T U K Z Q
W R X K X U O N X P I U P G F M Z U
W I Z I K T T Q P T D V O D Y G Q E
R D E L L V Z E R A Z I K Q U H E
A A O Y W X Z R S S E R T C A G Z N
J Y C Y G G C X Y K T C D P C H J S
I A E E V C L Z B Y Y F U B T Y D O
A F Q C S K X P L G J N U D O X O F
Z T R E A X H A K N Q A Q M O Y N C
V E G X A N U Q X V M I N O A R W O
U R C J N N L I J G Y D O C Y W P M
I N X J D U X R B B B E L B B I F E
H E L R X Z V C H Z C M Z V K Y H D
Z X Y R C P A A V B M O N Q K K D Y
J T P S Q B H E J T R C D K Y U P A
M O R R I S B R O W N C O L L E G E
A L G E B R A I N S T R U C T O R B
```

Find These Words

WRITER
COMEDIAN
ACTRESS
PRODUCER
ALGEBRAINSTRUCTOR

DIRTYLAUNDRY
SOULPLANE
FRIDAYAFTERNEXT
MORRISBROWNCOLLEGE
QUEENSOFCOMEDY

Directions: read and answer the questions. These are your opinions so the answers will vary.

Would you rather be famous for an invention or for telling jokes?

What's your favorite color?

Share a special memory you have from school.

Directions: read and answer the questions below. There are clues in the puzzle to help you. Try and solve the cryptic message. **Clue for cryptic message: Lori's family.**

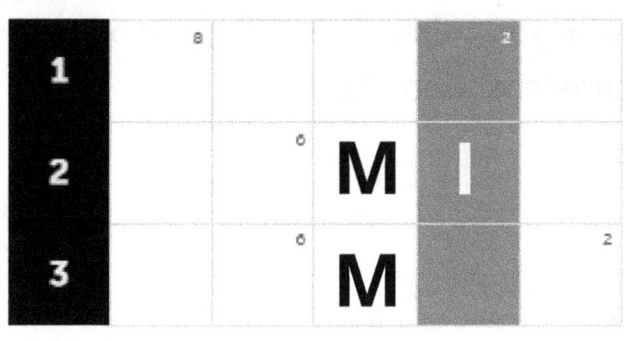

Questions

1) Sommore wrote and produced "The Queen Stands ____," a filmed version of her stand-up act, which debut on Comedy Central.
2) Sommore received the Richard Pryor Award for ___ of the Year.
3) Sommore was a featured comic in the "Latham Entertainment Presents" tour in 2002, where she was the only ___ performer.
4) Sommore hosted "Showtime at the ____."
5) Sommore hosted Russell Simmons' "Def ____ Jam."
6) Sommore was featured on the "Royal Comedy Tour" where she was the first female comedienne to Headline over other male ____ Headlining acts.
7) Sommore ____ fame by being the first woman to host BET's "ComicView."

97

Directions: This is the WGLT Challenge. Solve the cryptogram. As the puzzle solver, you need to find which number belongs to which character. And this can be pretty challenging! You will need to match the number with the letter. There are some letters given to you below. This will help you solve the other words and unlock more characters. **Good Luck.**

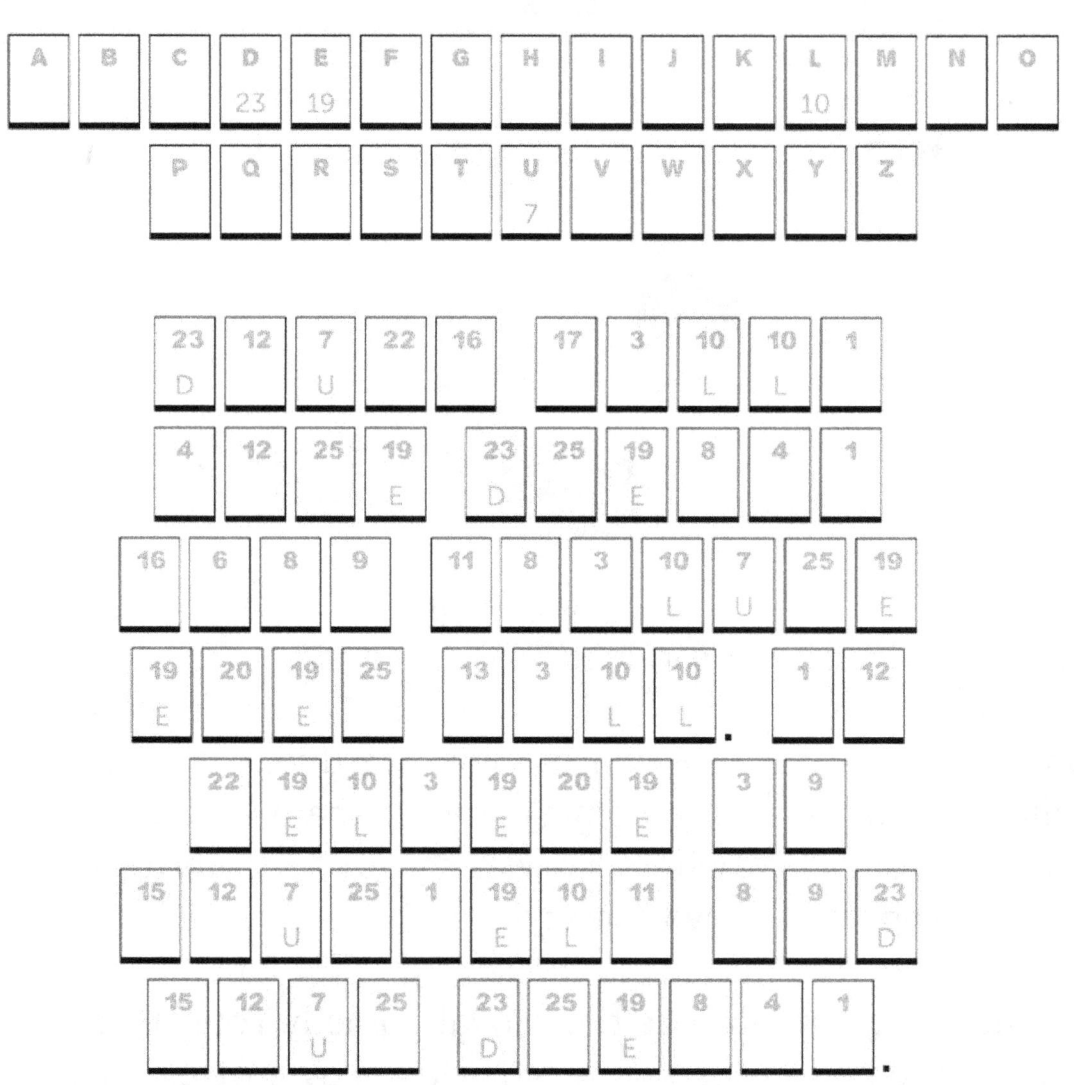

Solution key:
- A = 8, B = 22, C = ?, D = 23, E = 19, F = 11, G = ?, H = 6, I = 3, J = ?, K = 17, L = 10, M = 4, N = 9, O = 12, P = ?, Q = ?, R = 25, S = 1, T = 16, U = 7, V = 20, W = 13, X = ?, Y = 15, Z = ?

Decoded message:

DOUBT KILLS MORE DREAMS THAN FAILURE EVER WILL. BELIEVE IN YOURSELF AND YOUR DREAMS.

98

Broderick Harvey, Sr

January 17, 1957 – PRESENT
COMEDIAN / TV HOST

LEFT BLANK ON PURPOSE

Broderick Harvey, Sr

Broderick Harvey, Sr

Broderick Harvey, Sr

Broderick Harvey, Sr

Broderick Harvey, Sr

Broderick Harvey, Sr

Directions: read the bio below and answer the following questions.

Hi, my name is Broderick Stephen Harvey, Sr. I was born on January 17, 1957, in Welch, WV. I graduated from Glenville High School. I attended Kent State University and West Virginia University. I became a member of the Omega Psi Phi fraternity. In 1985, I made my comedy debut by performing at an open mic comedy night at the Hilarities Comedy Club. I brought the house down and the next day, I quit my job to pursue my dream. In 1990, I won a national comedy competition, which led to my big break: hosting Showtime at the Apollo. In 1993, I made my TV debut by hosting the Apollo. In 1997, I toured as one of The Kings of Comedy. In 2000, I started The Steve Harvey Morning Show, which is now syndicated in the United States. In 2003, I made my film debut in the movie The Fighting Temptations as Miles Smoke. In 2017, I began hosting the New Year's Eve special from Times Square for Fox. In 2022, I began hosting the arbitration-based court comedy Judge Steve Harvey on ABC.

1. What fraternity am I a member of?
    A. Omega Psi Phi
    B. Alpha Phi Alpha
    C. Kappa Alpha Psi
2. What year did I start doing comedy?
    A. 1990
    B. 1985
    C. 1993
3. What show of mine is in syndication through the U.S.?
    A. Showtime at the Apollo
    B. Kings of Comedy
    C. The Steve Harvey Morning Show

Directions: Answer the questions, to solve the crossword puzzle. You can use the internet if you get stuck on any question.

Across
3) Steve performed stand-up for the first time as part of an _____ night competition at a Cleveland nightclub.
4) Steve was offered national TV exposure on Showtime At _____ in 1993.
5) Steve is the author of Act _____, Think Like A Man published in 2009.
6) Steve has a _____ named the Steve Majorie Harvey Foundation which aims to "to provide outreach to fatherless children and young adult.

Down
1) The street Steve use to live on East 112th Street in _____ Ohio, was renamed to Steve Harvey Way.
2) Steve hosts The Steve Harvey Morning Show a _____ syndicated through the United States.

Directions: Read and answer the questions. These are your opinions so the answers will vary.

Would you rather play an individual or team sport?

What's your favorite Little Big Shots episode?

What goals do you have for yourself? What are 5 things you want to do before you are (21)?

Directions: Unscramble the words below about Steve. See if you can get the bonus word.

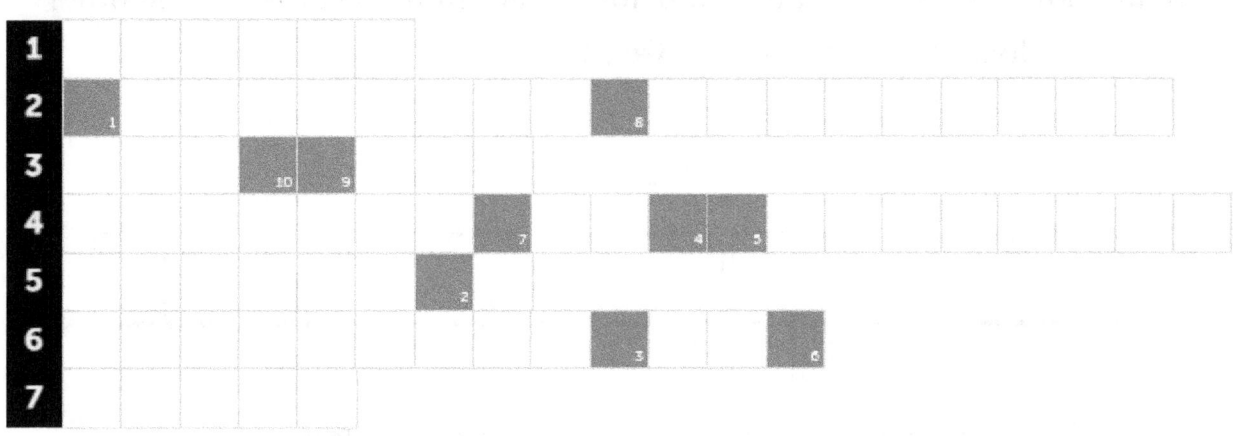

BONUS WORD

1	2	3	4	5	6	7	8	9	10

Unscramble Words

1) tovsht
2) fttintmgseonpaihtgi
3) crurpoed
4) sjovfyciahonnialmnot
5) mcnoidae
6) okgyisocmfned
7) ctaor

105

Directions: This is the WGLT Challenge. Solve the cryptogram. As the puzzle solver, you need to find which number belongs to which character. And this can be pretty challenging! You will need to match the number with the letter. There are some letters given to you below. This will help you solve the other words and unlock more characters. **Good Luck.**

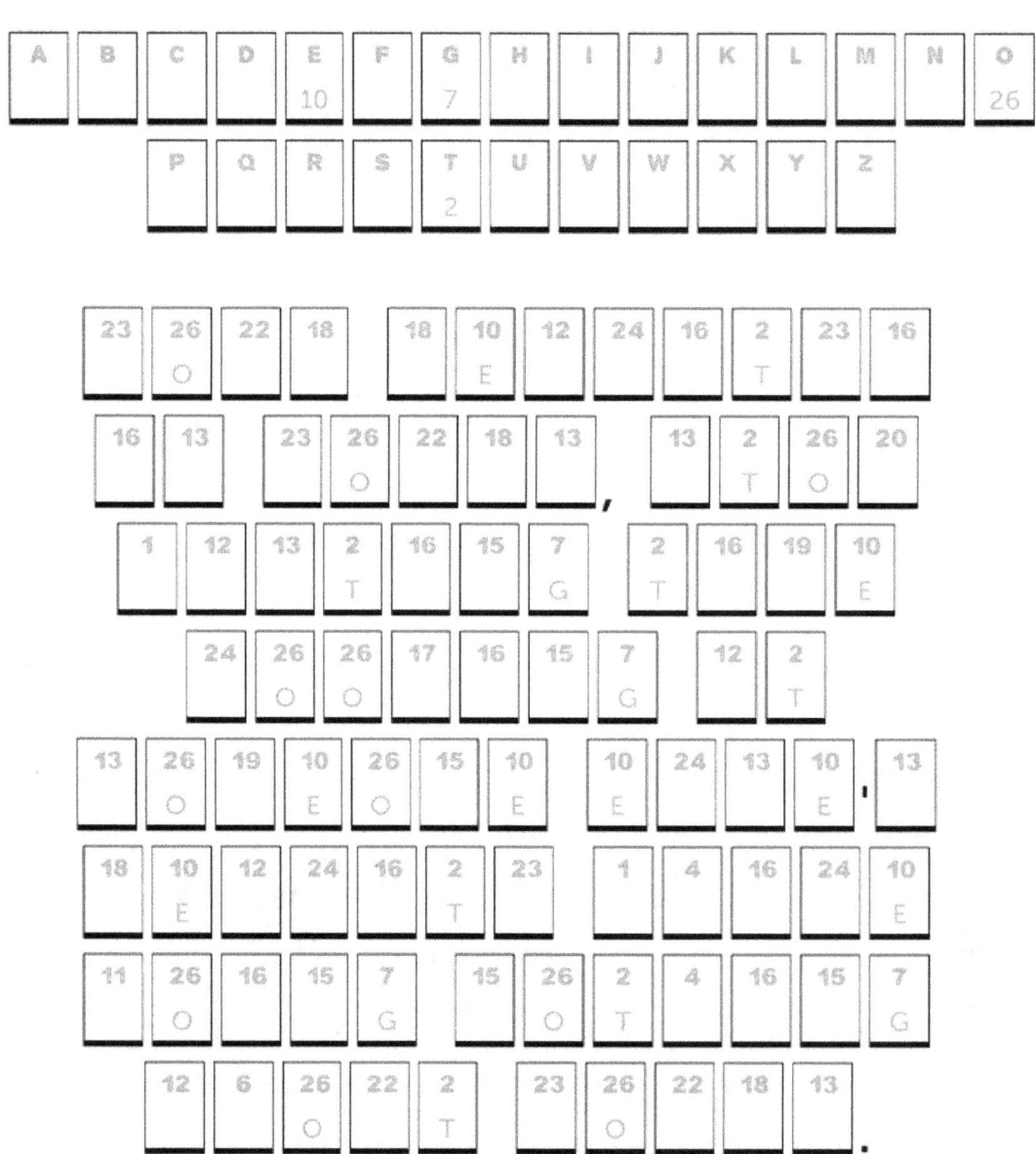

Broderick Dornell Smiley

Broderick Dornell Smiley

August 10, 1968 – PRESENT
COMEDIAN / RADIO PERSONALITY

107

LEFT BLANK ON PURPOSE

Broderick Dornell Smiley

Broderick Dornell Smiley

Broderick Dornell Smiley

Broderick Dornell Smiley

Broderick Dornell Smiley

Broderick Dornell Smiley

Directions: read the bio below and answer the following questions.

Hi, my name is Broderick Dornell Smiley. I was born on August 10, 1968, in Birmingham, AL. I graduated from Woodlawn High School. I received my Bachelor of Arts in Music from Alabama State University. I also became a member of the Omega Psi Phi fraternity while I was attending the university. My career began when I participated in an amateur comedy night at The Comedy Club. In 1992, I hosted BET's ComicView. In 1994, I performed at the Apollo Theater. I introduced the world to my prank phone calls using fictional characters whom I created; one of them was the famous Miss Bernice Jenkins. In 2000, I hosted ComicView again, and in 2001, I hosted the BET variety series The Way We Do It. In 2002, I appeared in Friday After Next as Santa. In 2004, I became the morning show personality for the radio station KBFB in Dallas. I also received the Platinum Mic Viewer's Choice Award at the BET Comedy Awards that year. In 2008, I signed a deal with Syndication One (a syndicated radio division of Radio One) to take my show nationwide.

1. What college did I get my Bachelors degree from?
    A. Tuskegee University
    B. Howard University
    C. Alabama State University
2. What fraternity do I belong to?
    A. Omega Psi Phi
    B. Kappa Alpha Psi
    C. Phi Beta Sigma
3. What award did I receive in 2004?
    A. Platinum Mic Viewer's Choice Award
    B. Network/Syndicated Personality of the Year
    C. Vision Award

Directions: Find the words associated with Broderick's life and career.

P	Z	J	T	O	D	Q	M	O	C	K	B	W	C	R	F	S	I
F	R	R	X	E	P	K	M	O	B	E	A	U	F	O	R	D	U
R	S	A	R	A	D	I	O	O	N	E	V	L	I	Y	O	N	B
I	L	S	N	A	M	P	S	I	Z	Q	Z	D	V	G	A	J	D
D	Y	N	A	K	E	G	D	Q	P	G	V	X	R	L	G	I	N
A	R	I	G	K	P	H	X	O	C	E	Q	F	M	A	W	U	Y
Y	A	K	S	S	T	H	G	H	Z	H	X	X	D	Z	X	E	P
A	D	N	W	N	K	N	O	X	T	R	N	F	Z	R	F	A	A
F	L	E	S	I	B	I	R	N	P	J	C	G	I	T	C	B	B
T	I	J	O	R	S	Z	U	L	E	O	E	Z	J	R	N	Z	T
E	L	E	D	I	F	T	S	M	T	C	G	S	O	L	A	H	F
R	J	C	W	M	Q	W	T	Q	I	G	A	T	T	K	I	Z	S
N	N	I	X	Y	K	Q	Y	Q	K	L	C	L	H	X	D	Y	Y
E	I	N	H	C	E	B	D	L	Z	A	V	Q	L	T	E	L	Q
X	B	R	F	G	E	G	A	X	H	K	L	W	T	S	M	E	O
T	O	E	G	V	I	J	L	Q	M	H	X	J	V	J	O	X	J
F	I	B	G	G	B	X	E	Z	Q	O	R	X	O	K	C	M	E
Q	Q	E	U	T	S	O	H	N	O	I	S	I	V	E	L	E	T

Find These Words

ACTOR
RUSTYDALE
TELEVISIONHOST
LILDARYL

BERNICEJENKINS
RADIOONE
FRIDAYAFTERNEXT

COMEDIAN
PRANKPHONECALLS
BEAUFORD

Directions: Read and answer the questions. These are your opinions so the answers will vary.

Would you rather text your friends or get together?

What's your favorite radio station or pod cast?

Describe a situation where you showed extra kindness toward a stranger or friend.

Directions: Read and answer the questions below. There are clues in the puzzle to help you. Try and solve the cryptic message.

Clue for cryptic message: Broderick had a show on this network.

Questions

1) Rickey is a featured _____ on the Fox-produced tabloid nationally-syndicated show Dish Nation.
2) Rickey hosted a season of BET's ____ in 2000.
3) In 2004, Rickey started being a morning show personality for ___ station KBFB in Dallas, Texas.
4) Rickey earned a bachelor's degree in ____ from Alabama State University.
5) Rickey has a reality television series about his life called Rickey Smiley For ____.

Directions: This is the WGLT Challenge. Solve the cryptogram. As the puzzle solver, you need to find which number belongs to which character. And this can be pretty challenging! You will need to match the number with the letter. There are some letters given to you below. This will help you solve the other words and unlock more characters. **Good Luck.**

114

DECEMBER 11, 1967 – PRESENT
COMEDIAN / ACTRESS

115

LEFT BLANK ON PURPOSE

Monique Angela Hicks

Monique Angela Hicks

Monique Angela Hicks

Monique Angela Hicks

Monique Angela Hicks

Monique Angela Hicks

Directions: read the bio below and answer the following questions.

Hi, my name is Monique Angela Hicks. I was born on December 11, 1967, in Woodlawn, Baltimore County, MD. I graduated from Milford Mill High School. I attended Morgan State University, but I graduated from the Broadcasting Institute of Maryland. I began my career in comedy during an open mic night at the downtown Baltimore Comedy Factory Outlet. In 1999, I made my TV debut in Moesha as Nicole "Nikki" Parker. Shortly after I made those appearances, a spin-off series was created surrounding my character, which was called The Parkers. In 2000, I made my film debut in 3 Strikes as Dahlia. In 2001, I toured as one of the queens in The Queens of Comedy. In 2009, I appeared in the film Precious. I received the AAFCA's Best Supporting Actress Award because I received the first-ever unanimous vote in an acting category and I also won the Academy Award for Best Supporting Actress for my role in Precious.

1. What college did I graduate from?
   A. Morgan State University
   B. University of Maryland
   C. The Broadcasting Institute of Maryland
2. What year did I get my own show?
   A. 1999
   B. 2000
   C. 2001
3. I won this award unanimously?
   A. Independent Spirit Award
   B. Academy Award for Best Supporting Actress
   C. AAFCA's Best Supporting Actress Award

Directions: Answer the questions, to solve the crossword puzzle. You can use the internet if you get stuck on any question.

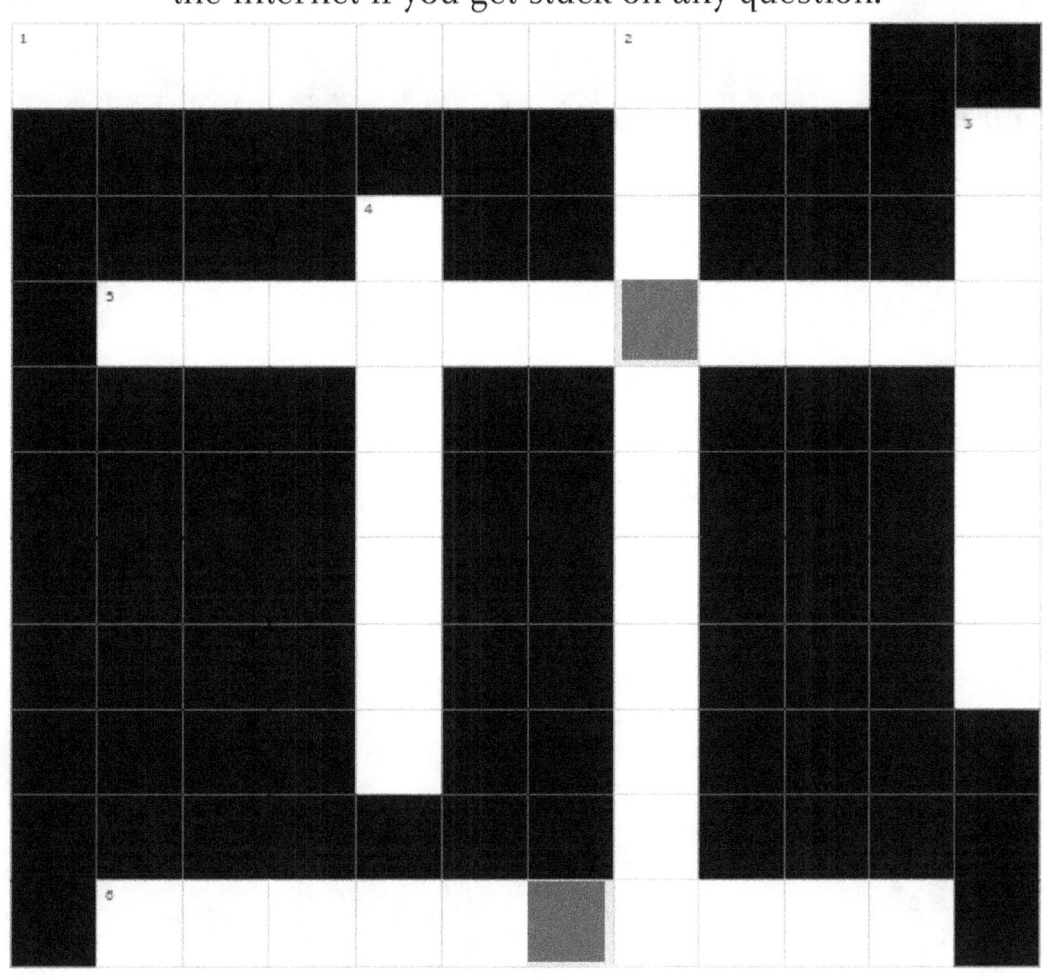

Across
1) Monique was the first woman, in 2002, to host the ___ show Showtime at the Apollo.
5) Monique owned a _____ in Baltimore, MD, in 1994 called Mo'Nique's.
6) Monique had her own ____: Mo'Nique in the Afternoon, on Radio One.

Down
2) Monique's first TV role was on the series _____.
3) In 2003, Monique was able to ___ her first book, Skinny Women Are Evil: Notes of a Big Girl in a Small-Minded World.
4) Monique created and starred in Mo'Nique's Fat Chance, the first ____-TV beauty pageant for full-figured women.

Directions: Read and answer the questions. These are your opinions so the answers will vary.

Would you rather be a wizard or a superhero?

What's your favorite video game?

Why do you think it is important to have rules in school?

Directions: Unscramble the words below about Monique. See if you can get the bonus word.

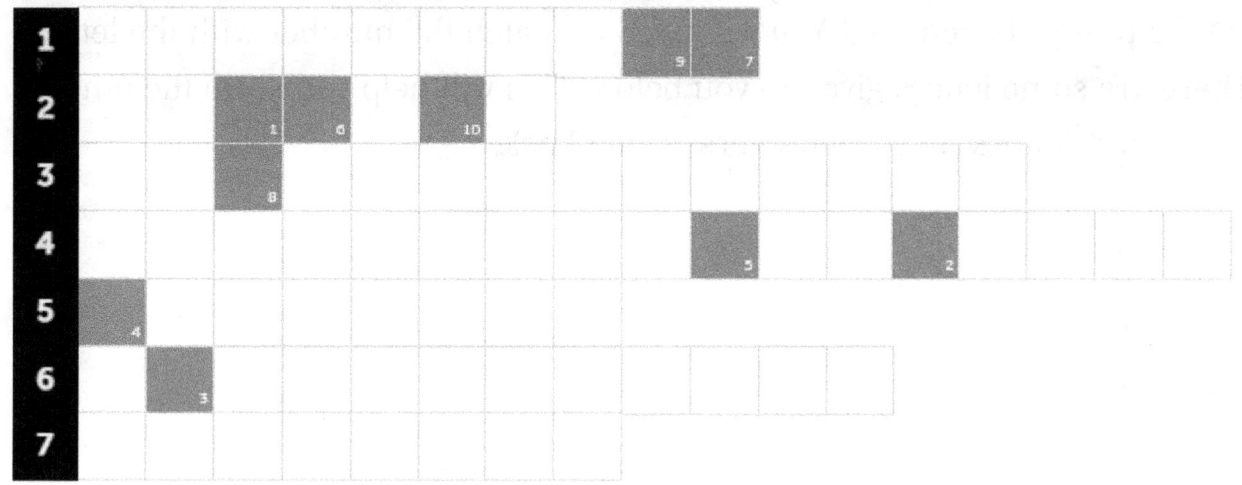

BONUS WORD

Unscramble Words

1) uotprkewnn
2) rsaesct
3) uysceonqdeeomf
4) fhosnemtiqeaaccnu
5) psruocie
6) jymeefodmcda
7) namoceid

Directions: This is the WGLT Challenge. Solve the cryptogram. As the puzzle solver, you need to find which number belongs to which character. And this can be pretty challenging! You will need to match the number with the letter. There are some letters given to you below. This will help you solve the other words and unlock more characters. **Good Luck.**

Richard Pryor

Richard Pryor

DECEMBER 1, 1940 – DECEMBER 10, 2005
COMEDIAN / ACTOR

LEFT BLANK ON PURPOSE

Richard Pryor

Richard Pryor

Richard Pryor

Richard Pryor

Richard Pryor

Richard Pryor

Directions: read the bio below and answer the following questions.

Hi, my name is Richard Franklin Lennox Thomas Pryor Sr. I was born on December 1, 1940, in Peoria, IL. I enlisted in the U.S. Army in 1958. In 1963, I went to New York to work at the clubs by performing my stand-up routines. Bill Cosby was my inspiration at this time. In 1966, I made my TV debut as Villar in The Wild, Wild West. In 1967, I made my film debut as Lt. Whitaker in The Busy Body. I acted in several TV shows over the years, such as The Ed Sullivan Show, The Johnny Carson Show and The Merv Griffin Show. In 1974, I co-wrote Blazing Saddles. In 1978, I starred in the film The Wiz. In 1980, I became the first Black actor to earn a million dollars for a single film when I was hired to star in Stir Crazy. In 1983, I signed a five-year contract with Columbia Pictures and I started my own production company, Indigo Productions. Over the next few years, I starred in Superman III, Brewster's Millions, Moving and See No Evil, Hear No Evil. In 1998, I won the first Mark Twain Prize for American Humor.

1. What branch of the service did I serve in?
   A. Air Force
   B. Marine Corps
   C. Army
2. I became the first black actor to?
   A. Earn a million dollars for five films
   B. Earn a million dollars for a single film
   C. Earn a million dollars for two films
3. I was the first person to win?
   A. Oscar
   B. Mark Twain Prize for American Humor
   C. Golden Globe

Directions: Find the words associated with Richard's life and career.

```
L A D Y S I N G S T H E B L U E S R
L F Y H S Z J K K T V E Z I W E H T
Y L H S I I P D R H N M I H I R H L
O I R U L M R W L W J A S X B G B G
H P B L V M Z E V O A T I H Q L J G
F W T X E Z T Y Q K E R C D Q Q I V
E I J F R R E T I R W E X A E C K D
Y L N U S R W M A S U D W N A M I Y
K S C D T O O D T T O L S N J B O M
M O E I R N R T Y F B I M Y F T Q C
A N Y C E G L G C D Q W L P Y X U Q
J S O Y A V O N C A I E Y W Q D S X
E H I B K T U F M X U N Y O X Q A P
B O D I P V P B R B Q E S T U L Y W
C W K U K W F G C C R G N Z H P Q W
B R E W S T E R S M I L L I O N S T
O Q E E R H T N A M R E P U S S T Z
U P I Y N S R H Y B H V P V I V R
```

Find These Words

ACTOR
COMEDIAN
WRITER
LADYSINGSTHEBLUES
BREWSTERSMILLIONS
SILVERSTREAK
SUPERMANTHREE
FLIPWILSONSHOW
THEWIZ
GENEWILDER

127

Directions: Read and answer the questions. These are your opinions so the answers will vary.

Would you rather play hide-and-seek or dodgeball?

Who's your favorite comedian?

What is one rule in all schools that you feel is unfair?

Directions: Read and answer the questions below. There are clues in the puzzle to help you. Try and solve the cryptic message.

Clue for cryptic message: One of Richard's movie.

Questions

1) Richard lived with multiple ___ for the last nineteen years of his life.
2) Richard co-wrote ___ Saddles but lost out on playing the lead role.
3) Rolling Stone and Comedy Central ranked Richard ___ on its list of the best stand-up comics of all time.
4) Richard won the Emmy for Best ____ in Comedy for the show "Lily."
5) Richard served in the US ___ for two years.
6) Richard was inspired by Bill ___ and use to perform with safe material until he had an epiphany at one of his shows in Las Vegas.
7) Richard made appearances on shows such as The Ed Sullivan ___ and The Tonight Show.

129

Directions: This is the WGLT Challenge. Solve the cryptogram. As the puzzle solver, you need to find which number belongs to which character. And this can be pretty challenging! You will need to match the number with the letter. There are some letters given to you below. This will help you solve the other words and unlock more characters. **Good Luck.**

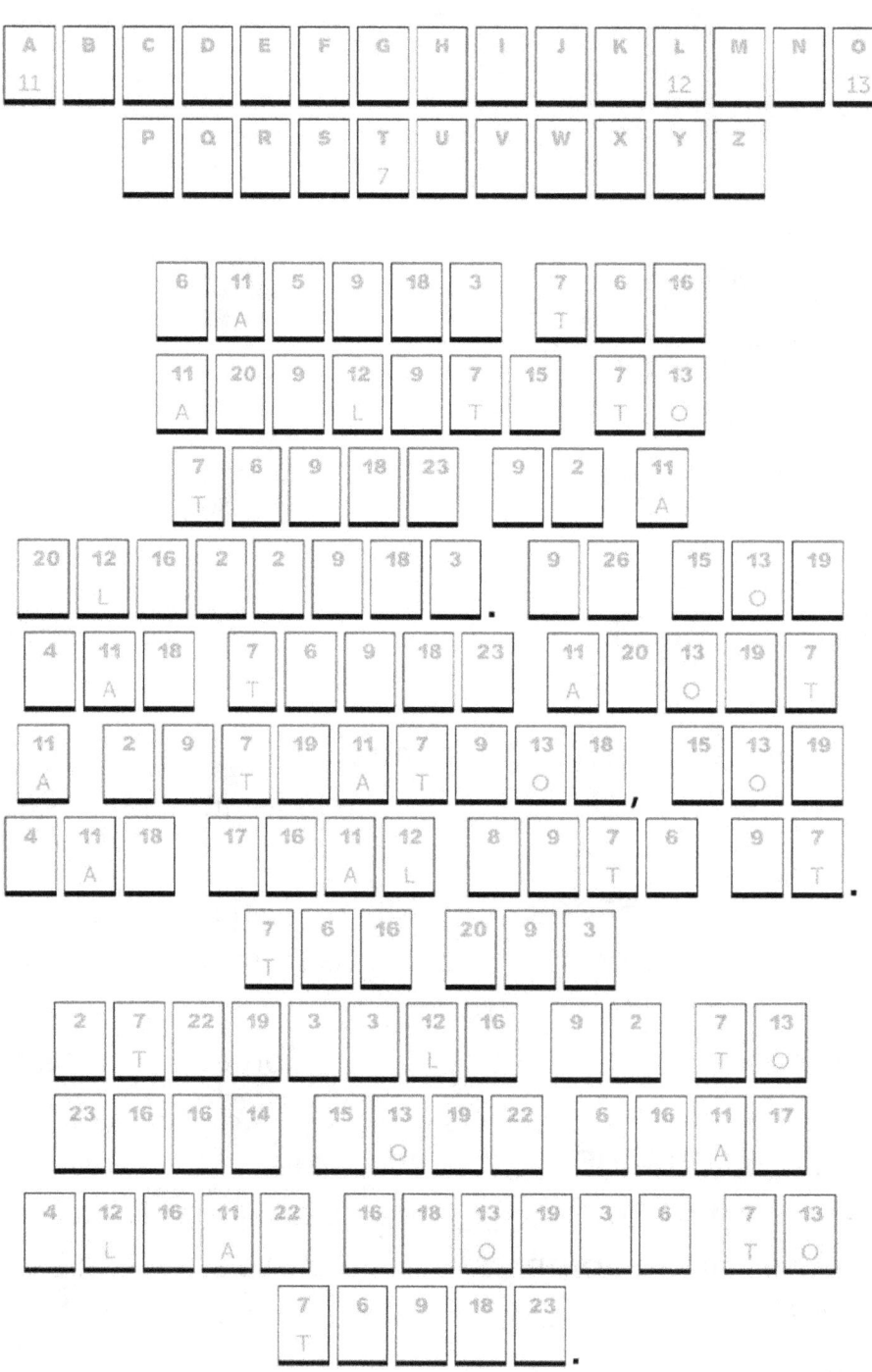

130

April 24, 1964 –PRESENT
COMEDIAN / ACTOR

131

LEFT BLANK ON PURPOSE

Cedric Antonio Kyles

Cedric Antonio Kyles

Cedric Antonio Kyles

Cedric Antonio Kyles

Cedric Antonio Kyles

Cedric Antonio Kyles

Directions: read the bio below and answer the following questions.

Hi, my name is Cedric Antonio Kyles. I was born on April 24, 1964, in Jefferson City, MO. I graduated from Berkeley High School. I earned my bachelor's degree from Southeast Missouri State University. In 1987, I made my TV debut on Showtime at the Apollo. In 1990, I won the Miller Lite Comedy Search. In 1993, I hosted ComicView. In 1996, I played Cedric Jackie Robinson on The Steve Harvey Show. That same year, I also toured and starred in The Kings of Comedy. In 1998, I made my film debut as Bo in Ride. I acted in several films and TV shows, such as Big Momma's House, The Proud Family, Ice Age, The Boondocks, the Barbershop franchise, Power, the Madagascar franchise, Summer Camp Island, Johnson Family Vacation, The Neighborhood, The Honeymooners and Black-ish.

1. What college did I get my Bachelors degree from?
    A. Missouri University
    B. Southeast Missouri State University
    C. Howard University
2. What year did I start doing films?
    A. 1987
    B. 1996
    C. 1998
3. Which film didn't I play in?
    A. Ice Age
    B. Madagascar
    C. The Proud Family

Directions: Answer the questions, to solve the crossword puzzle. You can use the internet if you get stuck on any question.

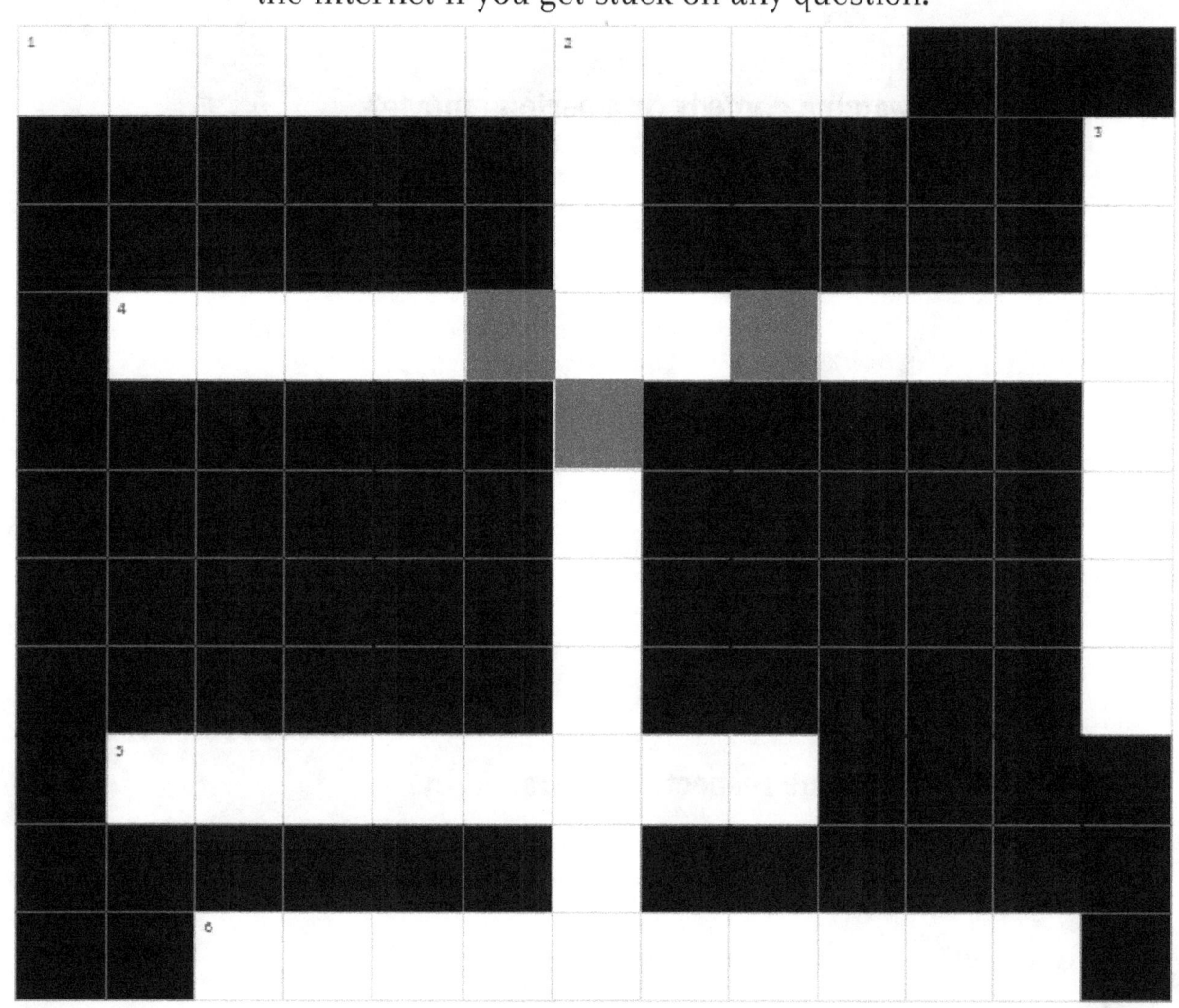

Across

1) Cedric was the host of the _____ game show Who Wants to Be a Millionaire.
4) Cedric received a star on the Hollywood _____.
5) Cedric first TV appearance was on _____ at the Apollo.
6) Cedric is the voice of Maurice the lemur in _____.

Down

2) Cedric is part owner Champ Car _____ series.
3) Cedric's favorite movie of all time is Coming to _____.

135

Directions: Read and answer the questions. These are your opinions so the answers will vary.

Would you rather watch a comedy or a serious movie?

What's your favorite activity to do with friends?

Do peers deserve the same respect as elders? Why?

Directions: Unscramble the words below about Cedric. See if you can get the bonus word.

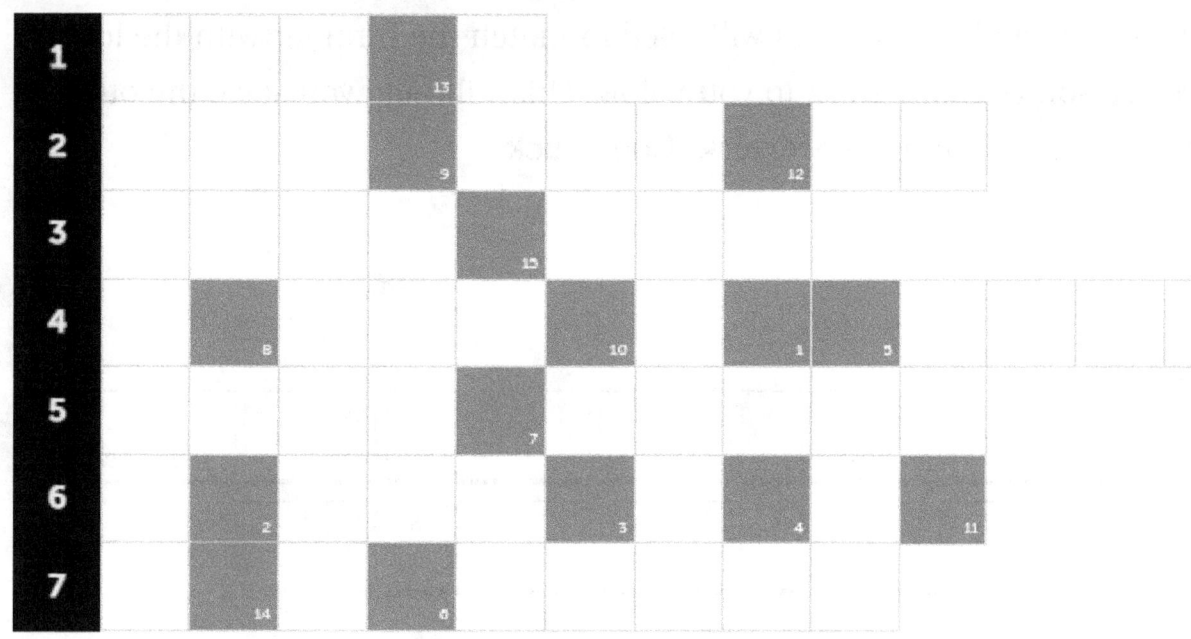

BONUS WORD

Unscramble Words

1) troac
2) brbasrepho
3) midneaoc
4) ocrtwehstebal
5) saacamdarg
6) anthcreele
7) moiicwcve

137

Directions: This is the WGLT Challenge. Solve the cryptogram. As the puzzle solver, you need to find which number belongs to which character. And this can be pretty challenging! You will need to match the number with the letter. There are some letters given to you below. This will help you solve the other words and unlock more characters. **Good Luck.**

December 3, 1979 –PRESENT
COMEDIAN / ACTRESS

LEFT BLANK ON PURPOSE

Tiffany Haddish

Tiffany Haddish

Tiffany Haddish

Tiffany Haddish

Tiffany Haddish

Tiffany Haddish

Directions: read the bio below and answer the following questions.

Hi, my name is Tiffany Sara Cornilia Haddish. I was born on December 3, 1979, in South Central Los Angeles, CA. I graduated from El Camino Real High School. In 2005, I made my TV debut in That's So Raven as Charlotte. I also made my film debut that same year in The Urban Demographic as Janice Green. I got my break in comedy in 2006 on Bill Bellamy's Who's Got Jokes. I have been performing in both avenues ever since. Here is a list of some of the TV shows and films that I have been in: Chelsea Lately, Meet the Spartans, That's So Raven, Janky Promoters, My Name Is Earl, Boosters, It's Always Sunny in Philadelphia, School Dance, The Underground, Nick Cannon's Short Circuitz, Keanu, Just Jordan, Girls Trip, In the Motherhood, The Lego Movie 2: The Second Part, Def Comedy Jam, The Secret Life of Pets 2, Reality Bites Back, Bad Trip, and New Girl.

1. What was the name of my High School?
   A. Charles Evans Hughes High School
   B. El Camino Real High School
   C. Morris High School
2. What year did I start my film debut?
   A. 2006
   B. 2005
   C. 2008
3. Which is not a film of mine?
   A. Bad Trip
   B. That's So Raven
   C. Girls Trip

Directions: Find the words associated with Tiffany's life and career.

T	V	Y	F	A	T	W	M	P	I	R	T	S	L	R	I	G	Z
P	F	O	S	T	E	R	C	A	R	E	W	J	R	Z	W	M	J
Q	N	K	O	I	C	B	G	D	X	G	T	H	F	U	W	N	M
A	B	K	D	L	M	D	K	H	A	P	N	K	S	B	X	Y	X
Q	B	M	S	Q	H	S	D	K	E	A	N	U	U	Y	T	C	U
K	R	J	H	S	I	S	D	N	E	T	F	L	I	X	H	O	Y
P	R	I	O	D	K	E	M	Y	Y	M	O	E	B	P	E	M	F
F	T	F	W	O	T	R	T	L	Y	N	R	T	R	U	F	E	R
D	L	C	T	N	B	T	G	R	M	D	F	V	S	I	C	D	G
J	A	Y	I	U	S	C	K	W	L	R	A	F	S	E	H	I	Y
N	D	L	M	E	P	A	R	P	N	D	Y	E	Z	W	V	A	N
Y	Z	S	E	G	D	W	B	N	C	W	I	K	R	H	Q	N	H
B	C	R	L	K	G	I	N	M	O	S	T	O	S	E	J	H	C
N	R	H	A	V	Z	T	I	M	K	C	A	L	B	D	H	M	C
M	I	E	R	F	S	X	W	G	Q	E	U	B	X	H	Z	S	F
Z	R	M	I	U	R	D	R	L	J	X	Y	C	G	Q	A	Z	D
U	B	E	S	T	C	O	M	E	D	Y	A	L	B	U	M	K	N
Y	I	V	J	U	E	D	L	E	D	W	T	Z	Z	J	B	D	A

Find These Word

ACTRESS
SHOWTIME
GIRLSTRIP
SHEREADY

NETFLIX
BESTCOMEDYALBUM
COMEDIAN

FOSTERCARE
BLACKMITZVAH
KEANU

Directions: Read and answer the questions. These are your opinions so the answers will vary.

Would you rather visit the mountains or the ocean?

What's your favorite show on TV?

Have you read The Last Black Unicorn? If so, what do you like about it?

Directions: Read and answer the questions below. There are clues in the puzzle to help you. Try and solve the cryptic message.

Clue for cryptic message: Tiffany talked about this from her childhood.

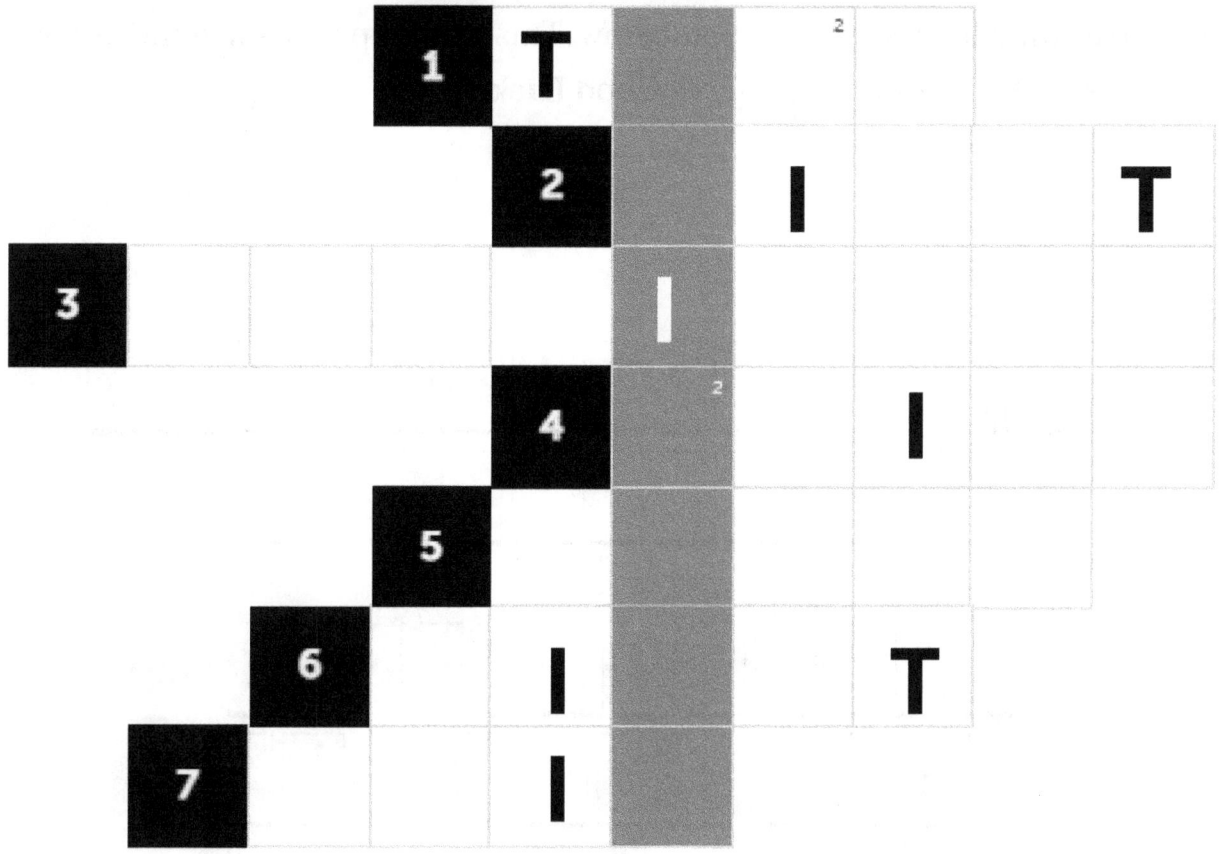

Questions

1) Tiffany is doing the voice over for Netflix's animated series called "___ and Bertie".
2) Tiffany was the first black female stand-up comic to host the Saturday ___ Live show.
3) Tiffany ___ A Best-Selling Book, Co-Written with Tucker Max.
4) Tiffany starred in the ___ comedy series The Afterparty.
5) Tiffany's first break was a spot on the comedy competition Bill Bellamy's Who's Got ___.
6) Tiffany's The Last O. G. is her ___ lead in a sitcom.
7) Tiffany uses comedy as an outlet for her ___.

Directions: This is the WGLT Challenge. Solve the cryptogram. As the puzzle solver, you need to find which number belongs to which character. And this can be pretty challenging! You will need to match the number with the letter. There are some letters given to you below. This will help you solve the other words and unlock more characters. **Good Luck.**

June 8, 1958 – PRESENT
COMEDIAN / FILM MAKER

LEFT BLANK ON PURPOSE

Keenen Wayans

Keenen Wayans

Keenen Wayans

Keenen Wayans

Keenen Wayans

Keenen Wayans

Directions: read the bio below and answer the following questions.

Hi, my name is Keenen Ivory Wayans. I was born on June 8, 1958, in Harlem, NY. I graduated from Seward Park High School. I attended Tuskegee University but left to pursue comedy. I went to LA to act in TV and films. In 1983, I made my film debut in Star 80 as a comic. That year, I also made my TV debut in the series For Love and Honor as Duke. In 1987, I helped write and produce Eddie Murphy: Raw. I also helped write Hollywood Shuffle and played Donald and Jheri Curl in the film. In 1988, I directed, wrote, and starred in I'm Gonna Git You Sucka. I played Jack Spade. In 1990, Fox gave me my own show. I wrote, starred in and created In Living Color, which was a sketch comedy TV series. Here are some more of the films that I either wrote, starred in, directed, or produced: A Low Down Dirty Shame, Don't Be a Menace to South Central While Drinking Your Juice in the Hood, The Glimmer Man, Most Wanted, Scary Movie, My Wife and Kids, Dance Flick, Happily Divorced and The Boo Crew.

1. What HBCU did I attend?
    A. Howard University
    B. Tuskegee University
    C. Fisk University
2. What did I help produce but didn't play a role in?
    A. White Chicks
    B. Most Wanted
    C. Eddie Murphy Raw
3. I created which comedy show in the 90's?
    A. The Fresh Prince of Bel-Air
    B. Martin
    C. In Living Color

Directions: Answer the questions, to solve the crossword puzzle. You can use the internet if you get stuck on any question.

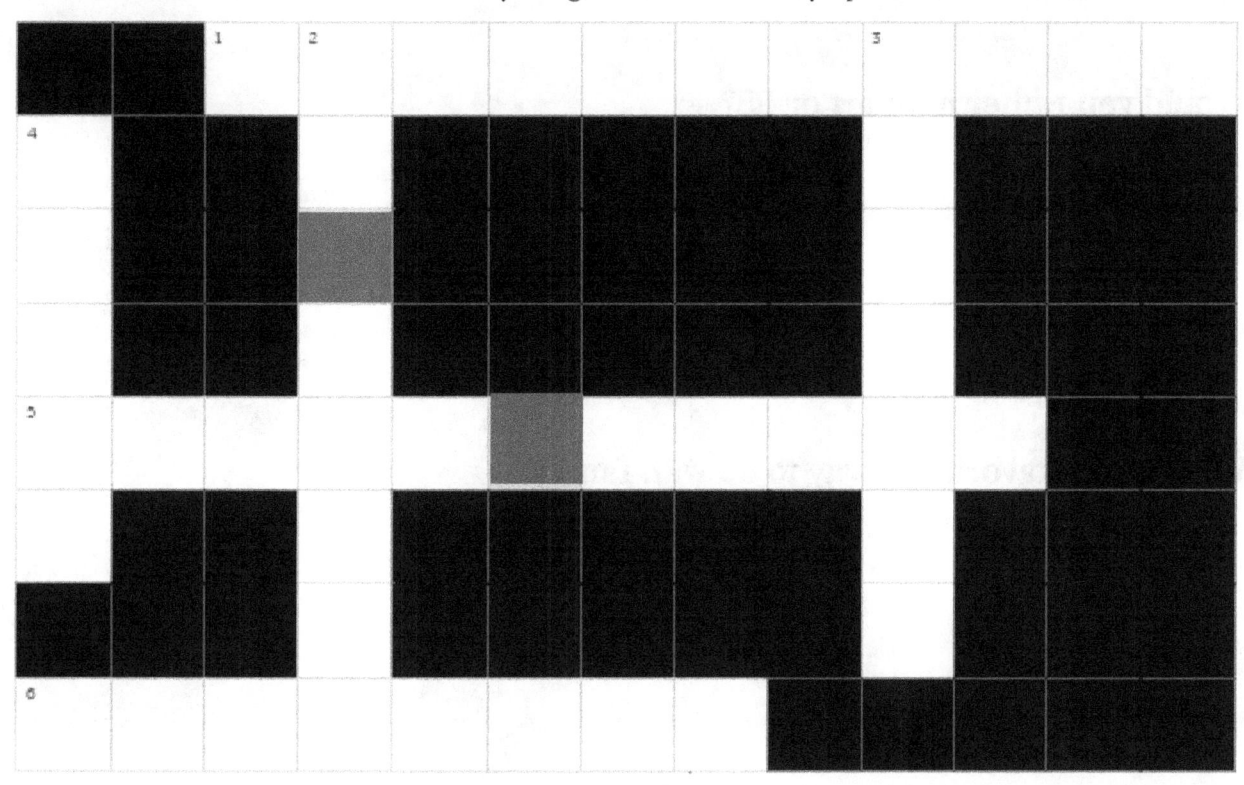

Across
1) Keenen got a ____ to study engineering at Tuskegee University in Alabama, but dropped out just one semester before graduation.
5) Keenen biggest success was the horror comedy ____, he also directed it.
6) Keenen ____ and wrote the 1988 classic 'I'm Gonna Git You Sucka.'

Down
2) Keenen directed and ____ with his brothers 'White Chicks', the sequel 'White Chicks 2'.
3) Keenen first regular role was as a ____ who wants to become a professional boxer in the television serial 'For Love and Honor'.
4) Keenen ____ major contribution to show business was when he played host and co-creator of sketch comedy series, 'In Living Color'.

Directions: Read and answer the questions. These are your opinions so the answers will vary.

Would you rather have art or PE?

What's your favorite activity to do with family?

Would you pick a comedy or scary movie to watch? Why?

Directions: Unscramble the words below about Keenen. See if you can get the bonus word.

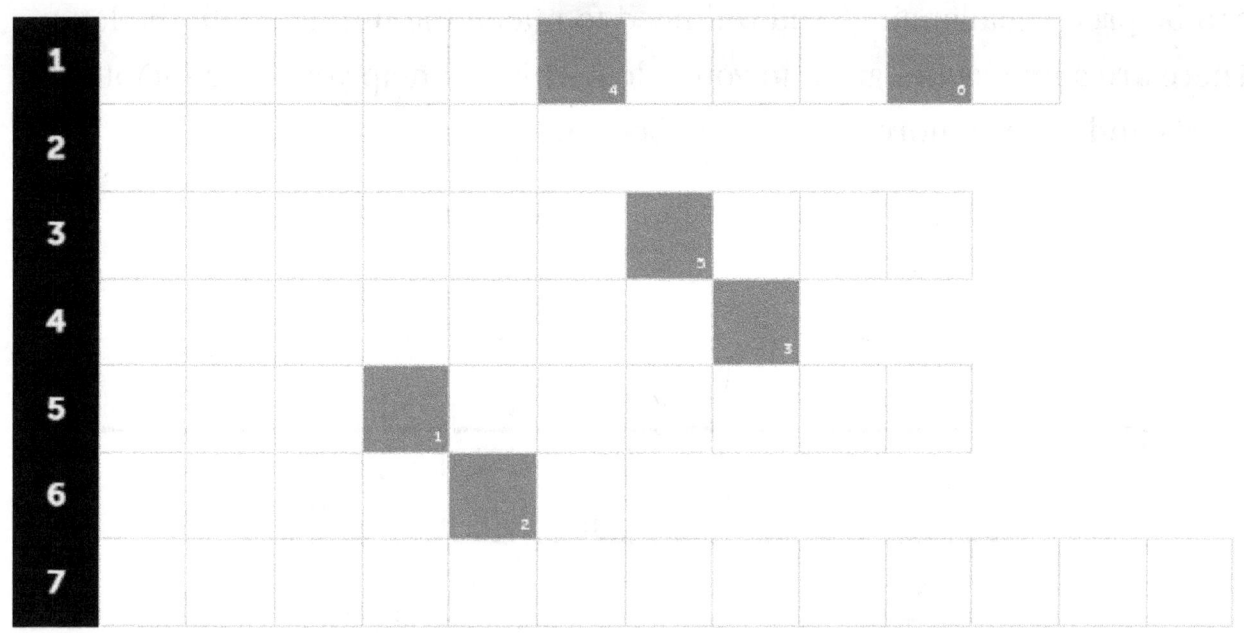

BONUS WORD

Unscramble Words

1) impissrosne 2) cator 3) syoracimev
4) oaedimnc 5) bhewctoreo 6) rietwr
7) rvngoncloliii

Directions: This is the WGLT Challenge. Solve the cryptogram. As the puzzle solver, you need to find which number belongs to which character. And this can be pretty challenging! You will need to match the number with the letter. There are some letters given to you below. This will help you solve the other words and unlock more characters. **Good Luck.**

154

Arsenio Hall

Arsenio Hall

February 12, 1956 – PRESENT
COMEDIAN / TALK SHOW HOST

LEFT BLANK ON PURPOSE

Arsenio Hall

Arsenio Hall

Arsenio Hall

Arsenio Hall

Arsenio Hall

Arsenio Hall

Directions: read the bio below and answer the following questions.

Hi, my name is Arsenio Hall. I was born on February 12, 1956, in Cleveland, OH. I graduated from Warrensville Heights High School. I got my bachelor's degree from Kent State University. In 1981, I made my TV debut on Soul Train as myself. In 1987, I made my film debut in Amazon Women on the Moon as an apartment victim. In 1988, I starred in Coming to America as Semmi, Extremely Ugly Girl, Morris and Reverend Brown. In 1989, Paramount contracted me to host a nationally syndicated late-night talk show, The Arsenio Hall Show. I became the first African American late-night host in the US. Some of the other TV and films I acted in are Harlem Nights, Madame's Place, Blankman, The Naked Brothers Band: The Movie, Thicke of the Night, Scooby-Doo! Pirates Ahoy, Martial Law, Black Dynamite, Real Husbands of Hollywood and Sandy Wexler.

1. What college did I get my Bachelors degree from?
   A. Ohio University
   B. Kent State University
   C. Cleveland State University
2. What year did I get my own late night show?
   A. 1987
   B. 1989
   C. 1988
3. I was the first African-American to do what in the U.S.?
   A. My Own Company
   B. My Own Late Night Show
   C. My Own Day Time Show

Directions: Find the words associated with Arsenio's life and career.

H	C	C	W	O	O	F	-	W	O	O	F	-	W	O	O	F	C	K
L	O	E	F	O	U	H	K	K	K	B	V	R	O	T	C	A	N	E
S	M	L	B	J	G	S	X	Q	E	V	X	J	T	Y	F	Z	Q	N
P	I	E	T	T	M	N	I	R	I	N	A	I	D	E	M	O	C	T
Q	N	B	J	W	A	H	A	K	Z	T	K	P	W	X	W	D	H	S
Y	G	R	A	R	S	E	N	I	O	H	A	L	L	S	H	O	W	T
I	2	I	R	D	N	O	O	J	S	Z	T	W	F	X	S	J	T	A
J	A	T	J	V	X	W	P	P	N	C	S	Y	B	E	G	M	N	T
X	M	Y	B	Q	G	G	A	D	A	M	O	Y	J	L	E	R	B	E
V	E	A	L	K	V	B	R	I	X	D	H	R	N	J	M	S	J	U
N	R	P	P	X	D	W	A	Y	W	F	W	Q	V	D	C	X	Z	N
X	I	P	I	L	V	P	M	Q	U	F	O	O	I	D	D	R	F	I
U	C	R	S	I	Q	O	O	V	Z	O	H	N	J	O	N	U	Q	V
I	A	E	V	M	A	Z	U	R	P	R	S	D	U	E	O	G	P	E
S	L	N	P	H	B	W	N	K	I	U	K	I	X	F	D	K	K	R
O	G	T	K	A	R	I	T	Y	K	G	L	Q	E	K	P	F	T	S
G	E	I	C	D	I	S	D	O	S	J	A	A	J	D	B	P	Y	I
U	Q	C	Y	K	S	F	B	Z	U	H	T	W	U	J	B	C	L	T
T	H	E	Q	H	A	R	L	E	M	N	I	G	H	T	S	Y	P	Y

Find These Words

TALKSHOWHOST
ACTOR
COMEDIAN
ARSENIOHALLSHOW
WOOF-WOOF-WOOF
COMING2AMERICA
CELEBRITYAPPRENTICE
HARLEMNIGHTS
KENTSTATEUNIVERSITY
PARAMOUNT

Directions: Read and answer the questions. These are your opinions so the answers will vary.

If you could work on a TV show or a series what would it be?

_____

_____

What state would you love to visit? Why?

_____

_____

Have you volunteered in your community? What did you do?

_____

_____

_____

_____

_____

Directions: Read and answer the questions below. There are clues in the puzzle to help you. Try and solve the cryptic message.

Clue for cryptic message: They used Arsenio's tag line in this movie.

Questions

1) Arsenio _____ "Arsenio Hall Presents Chunky A—Large and in Charge", a hybrid rap and comedy album.

2) Arsenio co-starred in the comedy ____ Coming to America.

3) Arsenio was the first African ____ to produce and host own show in 1989.

4) Arsenio went into ____ before pursuing a stand-up comedy career.

5) Arsenio had a Paramount contract to host a nationwide _____ late night talk show, The Arsenio Hall Show.

6) Arsenio had the leading role on the short-lived ____ Arsenio.

7) Arsenio was the announcer/sidekick for Alan Thicke during the short-lived talk show "Thicke of the ____."

Directions: This is the WGLT Challenge. Solve the cryptogram. As the puzzle solver, you need to find which number belongs to which character. And this can be pretty challenging! You will need to match the number with the letter. There are some letters given to you below. This will help you solve the other words and unlock more characters. **Good Luck.**

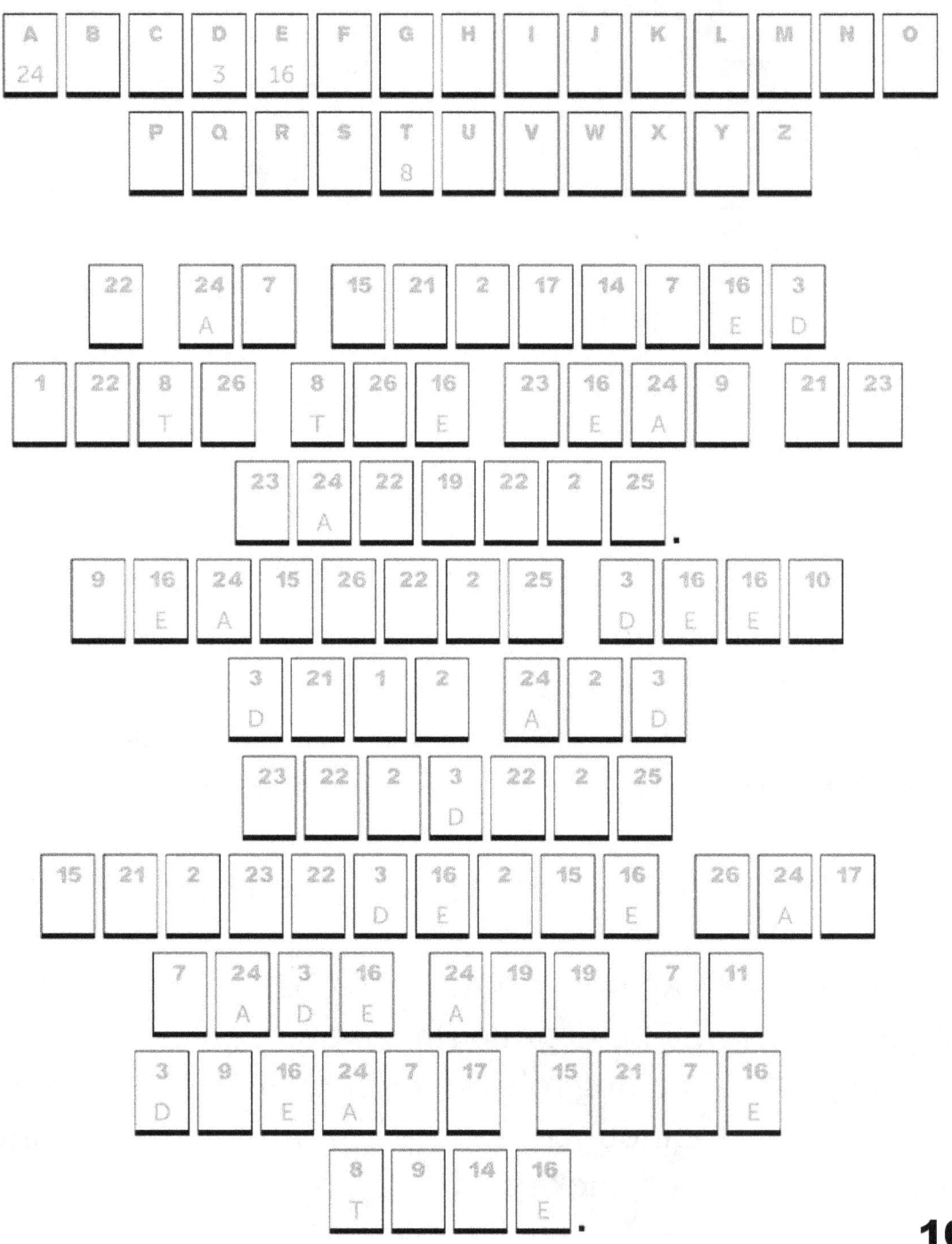

162

Annette Jones

Annette Jones

September 7, 1967 – PRESENT
COMEDIAN / ACTRESS

163

LEFT BLANK ON PURPOSE

Annette Jones

Annette Jones

Annette Jones

Annette Jones

Annette Jones

Annette Jones

Directions: Read the bio below and answer the following questions.

Hi, my name is Annette "Leslie" Jones. I was born on September 7, 1967, in Memphis, TN. I graduated from Lynwood High School. I attended Chapman University and Colorado State University for basketball. I started in comedy when a friend signed me up for a "Funniest Person on Campus" contest. I won and after that, I went to LA, where I started performing in comedy clubs. I performed on ComicView and at the Comedy Store. I toured with Jamie Foxx and Katt Williams. In 2013, I was hired by Saturday Night Live as a writer. By 2014, I was promoted to the cast as a featured act. Some of the TV shows and films that I have been in are For Love of the Game, In The House, Lottery Ticket, Coach, Top Five, Girlfriends, Trainwreck, Mind of Mencia, Ghostbusters, The Blacklist, Sing, Death to 2020, The Angry Birds Movie 2, Our Flag Means Death and Coming 2 America.

1. What college didn't I go to?
   A. UCLA
   B. Colorado State University
   C. Chapman University
2. How did I start doing comedy?
   A. Comedy Open Mic
   B. Funniest Person on Campus" contest
   C. Dare from my Dad
3. I use to work on this show?
   A. Saturday Night Live
   B. Key & Peele
   C. Martin

Directions: Answer the questions, to solve the crossword puzzle. You can use the internet if you get stuck on any question.

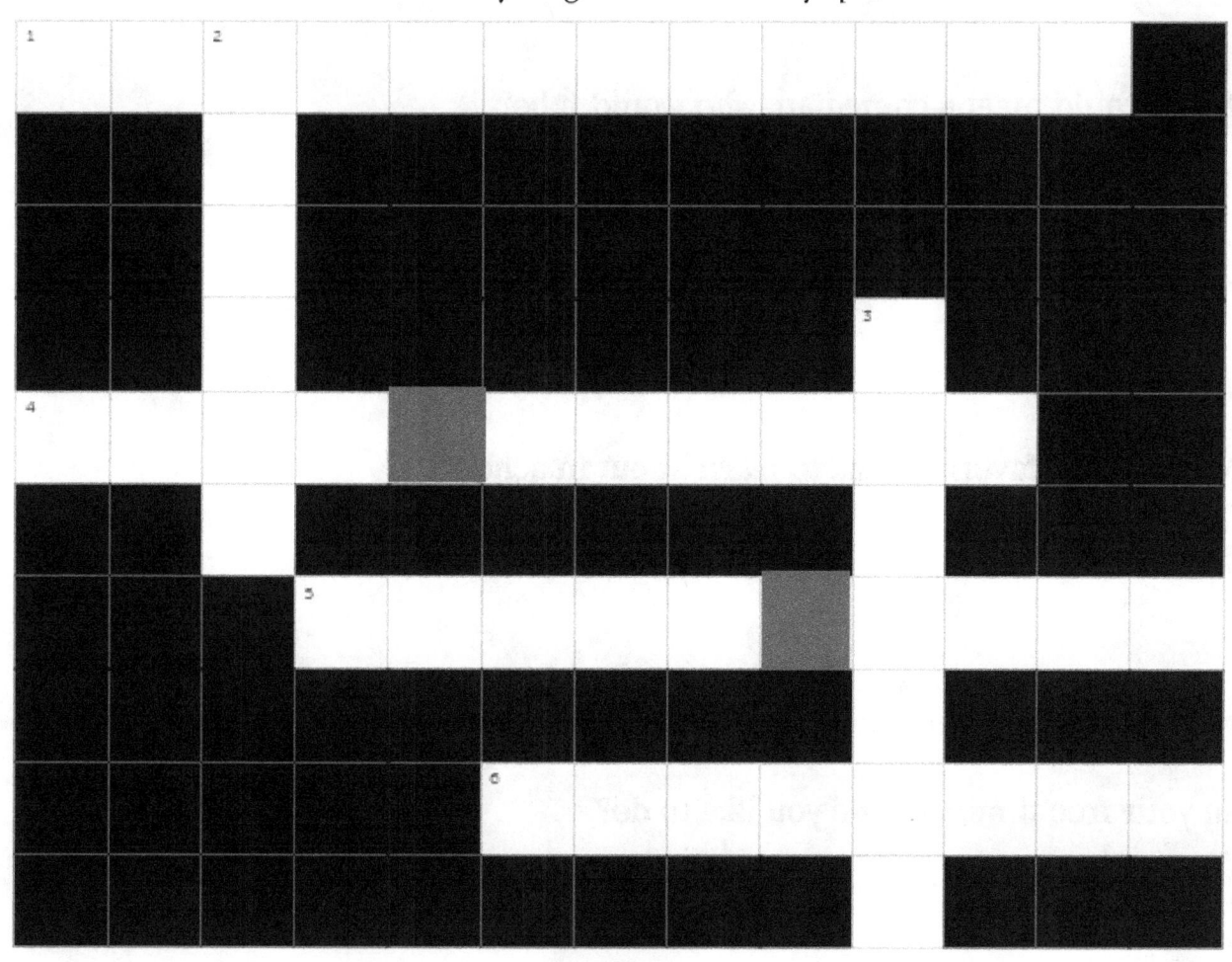

Across

1) Leslie starred in ____(2016) reboot as Patty Tolan.
4) Leslie worked as a ____ at the student radio station, KNAB at Chapman University.
5) Leslie toured with some of the top comics like ____ and Katt Williams.
6) Leslie got her start when she got entered into the ____ person on campus event and won.

Down

2) Leslie at age forty-seven became the ____ person to join Saturday Night Live as a cast member.
3) Leslie has a ____ special called "Time Machine".

Directions: Read and answer the questions. These are your opinions so the answers will vary.

If you could meet a comedian, who would it be?

_____

_____

What's your favorite thing to learn about in school?

_____

_____

In your free time, what do you like to do?

_____

_____

_____

_____

_____

Directions: Unscramble the words below about Leslie. See if you can get the bonus word.

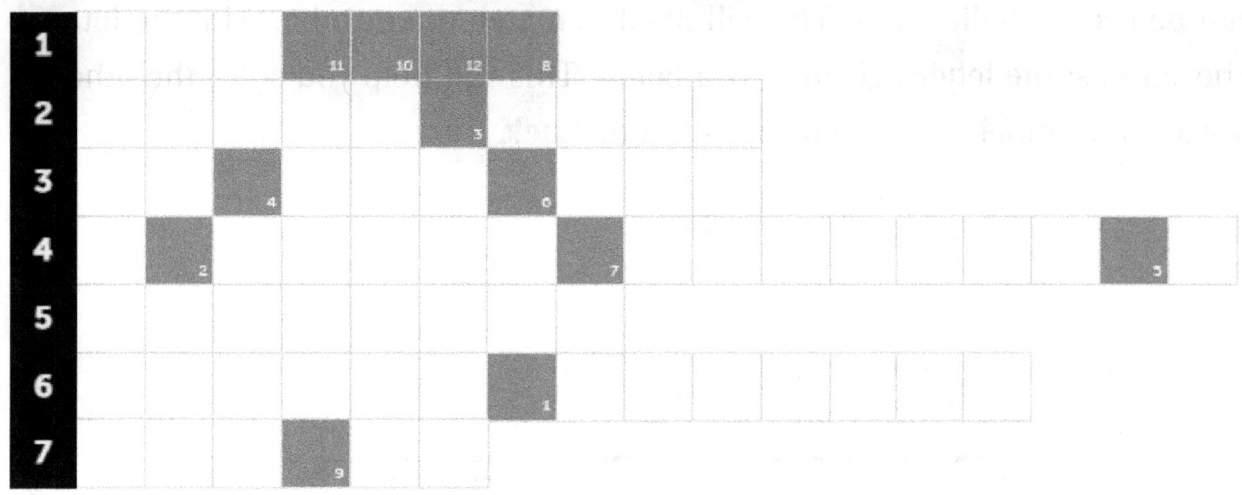

BONUS WORD

1	2	3	4	5	6	7	8	9	10	11	12

Unscramble Words

1) satersc
2) djcecsyoik
3) altselabbk
4) yrsmvaeiuatnihcnp
5) ocimdnae
6) glohgrdpiobewo
7) rtwrei

Directions: This is the WGLT Challenge. Solve the cryptogram. As the puzzle solver, you need to find which number belongs to which character. And this can be pretty challenging! You will need to match the number with the letter. There are some letters given to you below. This will help you solve the other words and unlock more characters. **Good Luck.**

Solution:

A	B	C	D	E	F	G	H	I	J	K	L	M	N	O
26	18	2	18	25		3	21	14		24		10	20	17

P	Q	R	S	T	U	V	W	X	Y	Z
11		6	22	15	1	9	4		13	

Message:

YOU CAN ACHIEVE YOUR DREAMS AT ANY AGE. SO KEEP WORKING TOWARDS THEM.

170

Martin Lawrence

Martin Lawrence

April 16, 1965 – PRESENT
COMEDIAN / ACTOR

171

LEFT BLANK ON PURPOSE

Martin Lawrence

Martin Lawrence

Martin Lawrence

Martin Lawrence

Martin Lawrence

Martin Lawrence

Directions: read the bio below and answer the following questions.

Hi, my name is Martin Lawrence. I was born on April 16, 1965, in Frankfurt, West Germany. I graduated from Friendly High School. I was a Mid-Atlantic Golden Gloves boxing contender before I went into comedy. I performed at The Improv before receiving a spot on Star Search. In 1987, I debuted on TV by playing Maurice Warfield in the show What's Happening Now. In 1989, I made my film debut by playing Cee in Do the Right Thing. In 1990, I played Bilal in House Party 1 and 2. In 1992, I became the host of the biggest comedy show for African-American comedians at the time, which was Russell Simmons' Def Comedy Jam. That year, I also got my own show, Martin, on the Fox network. Some more of the TV shows and films that I acted in are Bad Boys, Hammer, Slammer, G Slade, A Thin Line Between Love and Hate, Saturday Night Live, Life, Partners, Big Momma's House, National Security and Welcome Home Roscoe Jenkins.

1. What did I do before I started comedy?
    A. Computer Programming
    B. Golden Gloves boxing
    C. Teacher
2. What year did I start doing films?
    A. 1987
    B. 1989
    C. 1990
3. Which show did I create and star in?
    A. Star Search
    B. Martin
    C. Def Comedy Jam

Directions: Find the words associated with Martin's life and career.

```
O N U Q H X U Z L Z L O W T J C K E
Z O J N I T R A M U T C V Y K J D Q
A R C L Y G C O Z N K K C C Q Z P D
I I O L X B G T R X D J B Y Z I P G
H K M H J Z P R R O T C E R I D S F
A M E B A D B O Y S 2 W Y T W I G W
E M D W B S L C U A U O H M H C O N
D Q I F M Z T P Q I M G T G O X D U
F T A Y O B S F T C I S N N U C D I
K G N Q D F G C L N X K I A S X L H
C W T V Z V K Y K C L L C R E A I Q
T O J T F V Z K T C Q T I E P R W F
F V F K V S C S R O N M D M A Q Z B
U W T K K A E D T F A C T O R S R I
C K Q X L B G B R L Q H F O T M S M
U Q N B G D Y C V R H X Z B Y P I Q
D B I G M O M M A S H O U S E I S G
X I Q P G V Q C S B C B X U Y O V M
```

Find These Words

DIRECTOR   BLACKKNIGHT
COMEDIAN   BADBOYS2
ACTOR   BIGMOMMASHOUSE
MARTIN   WILDDOGS
HOUSEPARTY   BOOMERANG

Directions: Read and answer the questions. These are your opinions so the answers will vary.

If you could meet a historical figure, who would it be?

What's your favorite extracurricular class?

What is your favorite Martin film? Why?

Directions: Read and answer the questions below. There are clues in the puzzle to help you. Try and solve the cryptic message.

Clue for cryptic message: One of Martin's movies.

Questions

1) Martin made his directorial debut with his film "A Thin Line _____ Love and Hate."

2) Martin at eighteen appeared on an episode of Star _____ and did some of his first-ever comedy in front of a live audience but he didn't win.

3) Martin was a Mid-Atlantic _____ Gloves contender at fifteen years old.

4) ___ James teamed up with Nike to make Martin Lawrence-themed sneakers from his show "Martin."

5) Martin gets _____ performing stand-up but they're good nerves by keeping him focused on the task at hand.

6) Martin was named after Martin Luther King and President _____.

7) Martin worked as a telephone salesman for _____ alongside the rapping duo Salt-N-Pepa.

Directions: This is the WGLT Challenge. Solve the cryptogram. As the puzzle solver, you need to find which number belongs to which character. And this can be pretty challenging! You will need to match the number with the letter. There are some letters given to you below. This will help you solve the other words and unlock more characters. **Good Luck.**

Kevin Hart

Kevin Hart

July 6, 1979 – PRESENT
COMEDIAN / ACTOR

179

LEFT BLANK ON PURPOSE

Kevin Hart

Kevin Hart

Kevin Hart

Kevin Hart

Kevin Hart

Kevin Hart

Directions: read the bio below and answer the following questions.

Hi, my name is Kevin Hart. I was born on July 6, 1979, in Philadelphia, PA. I graduated from George Washington High School. I began performing standup comedy at The Laff House in Philadelphia. It took a little while for my comedy standup to become recognized, but in the meantime, I was still making moves. In 2002, I made my TV and film debuts. I was in the TV sitcom Undeclared as Luke and my first film was Paper Soldiers. I played the character Shawn. While I was polishing my comedy standup, I acted in several films and TV shows: Scary Movie 3, The Big House, Soul Plane, Barbershop, The 40-Year-Old Virgin, Wild 'n Out and Epic Movie. After a few years of acting, I felt that my standup was ready. I started to put in the work to solidify myself as an all-time great in the comedy world. In 2009, I founded HartBeat Productions. I also released Kevin Hart: I'm a Grown Little Man and my career blew up in a major way. In 2010, I released Kevin Hart: Seriously Funny, which was even more popular than my last comedy special.

1. What was the name of my High School?
   A. George Washington High School
   B. Barack Obama Green Charter High School
   C. John F. Kennedy High School
2. What year did I start acting and TV?
   A. 2000
   B. 2002
   C. 2004
3. I founded what company in 2009?
   A. Help From the Hart Charity (HFTH)
   B. Laugh Out Loud
   C. HartBeat Productions

Directions: Answer the questions, to solve the crossword puzzle. You can use the internet if you get stuck on any question.

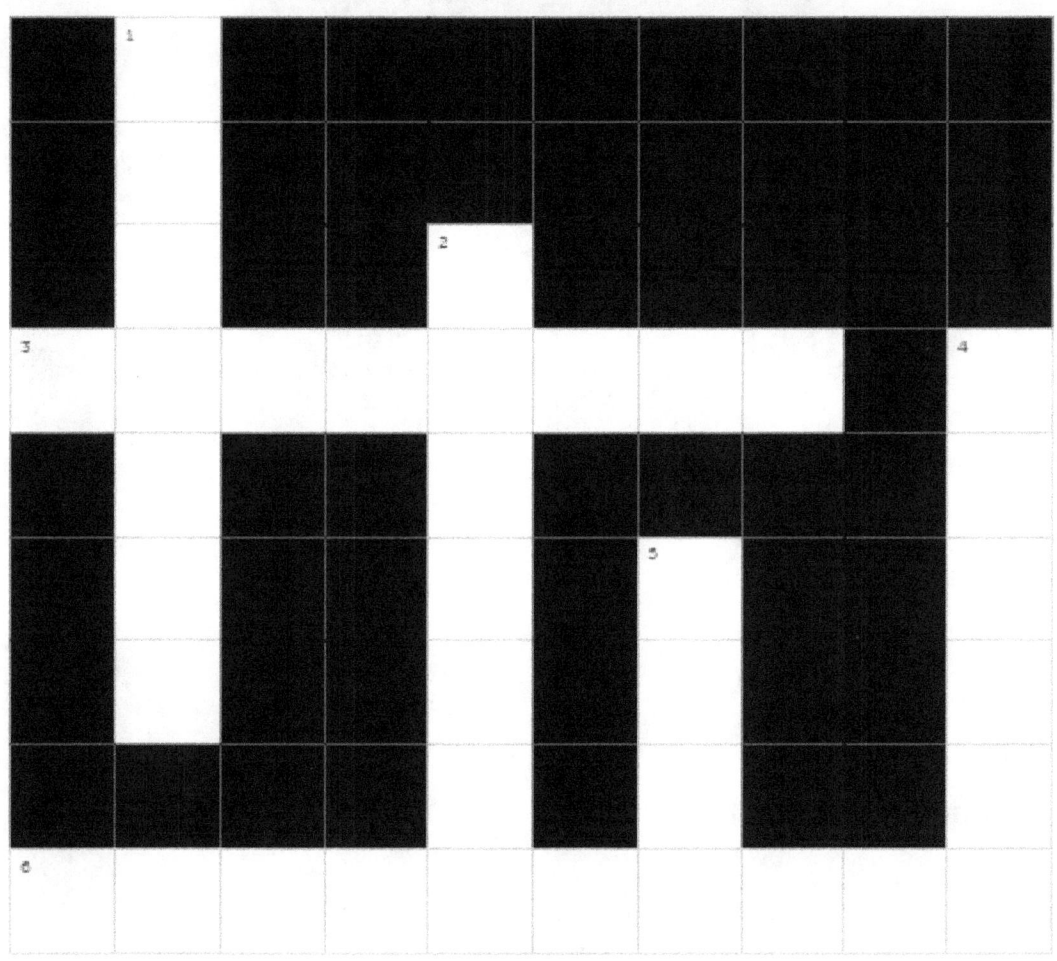

Across
3) Kevin uses a lot of his ____ life experiences in his comedy shows.
6) Kevin debuted a ____ restaurant called Hart House in Los Angeles, California, in 2022.

Down
1) Kevin founded Laugh Out Loud Productions, a global media and production company to provide opportunities for top ____ talent of all ethnicities worldwide.
2) Kevin has his own ____ called Comedy Gold Minds.
4) Kevin's alias Chocolate Droppa, is signed to ____ Records and released Kevin Hart: What Now mixtape.
5) Kevin won the MVP award ____ straight years in a row at the NBA All-Star Celebrity Game.

Directions: Read and answer the questions. These are your opinions so the answers will vary.

If you could go back to any period in time, which would you choose?

What's your favorite Kevin animation film?

What is a unique talent you have?

184

Directions: Unscramble the words below about Kevin. See if you can get the bonus word.

BONUS WORD

Unscramble Words

1) midacoen   **2)** tleipaneemxl   **3)** trcoa
4) nwoahwt   **5)** poanlelsu   **6)** indorlgea
7) cueiebc

185

Directions: This is the WGLT Challenge. Solve the cryptogram. As the puzzle solver, you need to find which number belongs to which character. And this can be pretty challenging! You will need to match the number with the letter. There are some letters given to you below. This will help you solve the other words and unlock more characters. **Good Luck.**

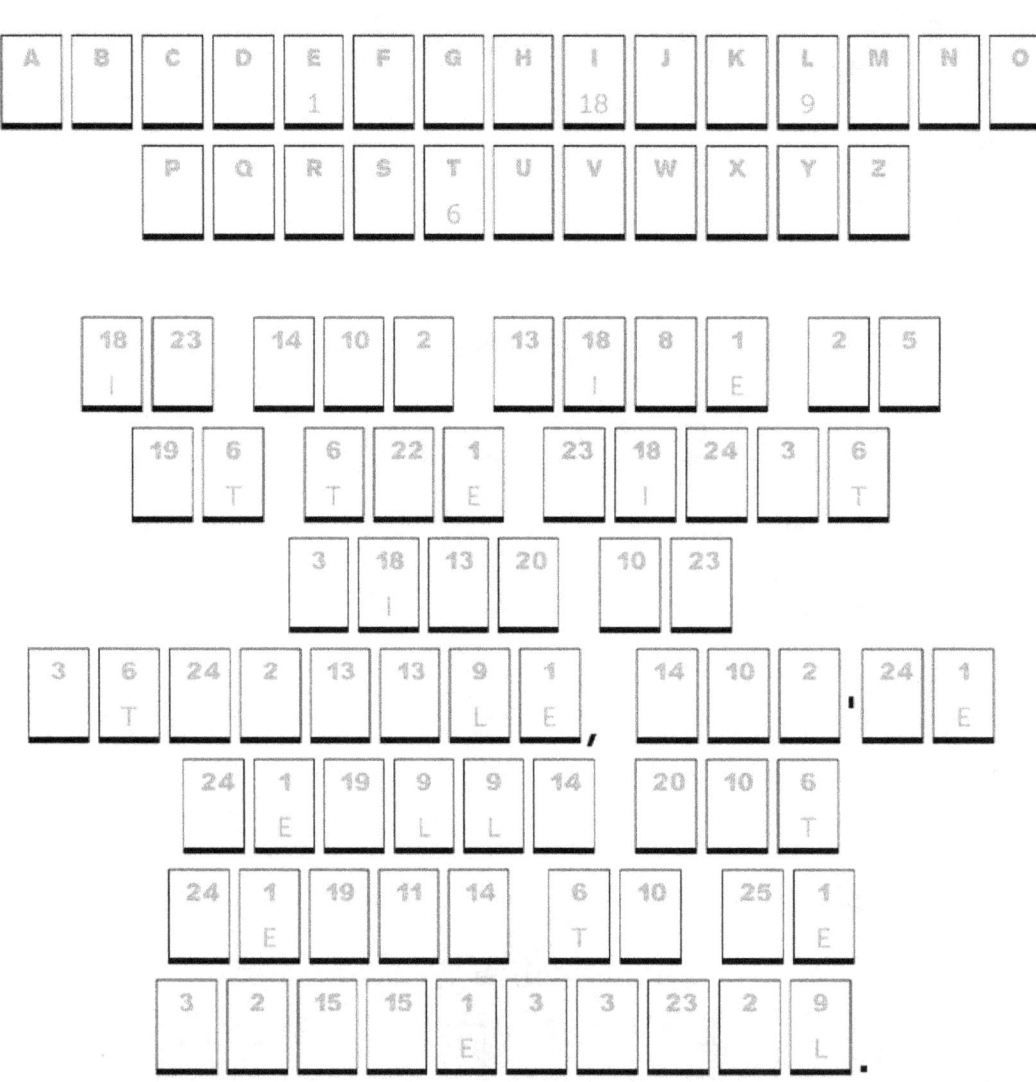

186

Jordan Peele

Jordan Peele

February 21, 1979 – PRESENT
COMEDIAN / FILMMAKER

LEFT BLANK ON PURPOSE

Jordan Peele

Jordan Peele

Jordan Peele

Jordan Peele

Jordan Peele

Jordan Peele

Directions: read the bio below and answer the following questions.

Hi, my name is Jordan Peele. I was born on February 21, 1979, in New York City, NY. I graduated from The Calhoun School. I started regularly performing at Boom Chicago in Amsterdam and The Second City in Chicago. In 2003, I made my TV debut on Mad TV as a writer and actor. In 2008, I made my film debut by playing D-Rock Peppers in Boner Boyz. Some of the other TV shows and films that I acted in before making my director's debut are Little Fockers, Chocolate News, Wanderlust, Reno 911, The Sidekick, SuperNews, Keanu, and Key and Peele. In 2017, I made my director debut with the film Get Out. I received four nominations at the 90th Academy Awards for Best Picture, Best Director and Best Original Screenplay. I won the Academy Award for Best Original Screenplay, which made me the first African American screenwriter to win in this category. I also was the first Black person to be nominated for Best Picture, Best Director and Best Original Screenplay for a debut film.

1. Where didn't I start out performing at?
   A. Boom Chicago
   B. The Second City
   C. Mad TV
2. What year did I start doing Directing?
   A. 2008
   B. 2017
   C. 2003
3. I was the first African-American screenwriter to win?
   A. Golden Globe for Best Original Screenplay
   B. Academy Award for Best Original Screenplay
   C. Emmy for Best Original Screenplay

Directions: Find the words associated with Jordan's life and career.

H	K	K	N	I	C	M	I	I	E	J	C	O	I	C	T	N	F
C	O	M	E	D	I	A	N	E	N	G	M	Z	I	U	B	Q	R
U	L	O	V	E	C	R	A	F	T	C	O	N	T	R	Y	I	Y
O	L	A	N	S	R	D	U	Q	J	J	P	F	E	H	X	B	C
G	C	X	E	N	O	Z	T	H	G	I	L	I	W	T	E	H	T
U	T	M	R	R	T	V	Q	C	O	G	R	A	F	Q	G	O	W
M	D	X	S	Y	C	I	M	S	M	E	G	A	U	D	F	L	L
S	Y	C	O	R	A	F	U	V	S	D	A	I	B	N	I	D	D
Y	N	K	I	R	S	I	C	X	H	P	S	G	Z	A	A	V	C
H	X	A	X	M	R	H	E	B	Q	N	U	W	I	D	W	E	D
X	Y	Z	Y	S	H	R	E	K	A	M	M	L	I	F	N	W	K
I	O	G	L	H	G	O	T	S	A	L	E	H	T	I	I	D	P
B	Y	B	J	Q	C	L	S	V	R	O	R	U	Y	M	E	B	O
S	H	P	B	M	D	K	E	Y	A	N	D	P	E	E	L	E	E
S	T	D	U	Y	S	T	P	C	P	F	W	V	A	Y	K	R	Z
S	Y	U	X	S	F	B	E	L	Z	K	O	Z	E	L	R	Z	O
V	U	O	X	P	G	G	M	A	T	M	R	Z	R	K	P	Q	Y
H	O	S	C	A	R	F	F	Y	G	W	X	J	F	H	X	V	Z

Find These Words

FILMMAKER   KEANU   COMEDIAN
THETWILIGHTZONE   KEYANDPEELE   ACTOR
FARGO   THELASTOG   LOVECRAFTCONTRY
OSCAR

Directions: Read and answer the questions. These are your opinions so the answers will vary.

If you could meet a cartoon character in real life, who would you pick?

Who is a friend at school that you know you can count on?

What is one thing you want to know about your teacher?

Directions: Read and answer the questions below. There are clues in the puzzle to help you. Try and solve the cryptic message.

Clue for cryptic message: One of Jordan's movies.

Questions

1) Jordan co-starred with ___-Michael Key on there hit sketch-comedy series "Key and Peele."
2) Jordan was a ___ for Spike Lee's BlacKkKlansman film.
3) Jordan was interested in making films since he was around ____ years old.
4) Jordan produced the ___ series Lovecraft Country.
5) Jordan co-produced and co-wrote the 2021 ___ to Candyman, using his Monkeypaw Productions Company.
6) Jordan won an Emmy for his MADtv song Sad 50 ____.

Directions: This is the WGLT Challenge. Solve the cryptogram. As the puzzle solver, you need to find which number belongs to which character. And this can be pretty challenging! You will need to match the number with the letter. There are some letters given to you below. This will help you solve the other words and unlock more characters. **Good Luck.**

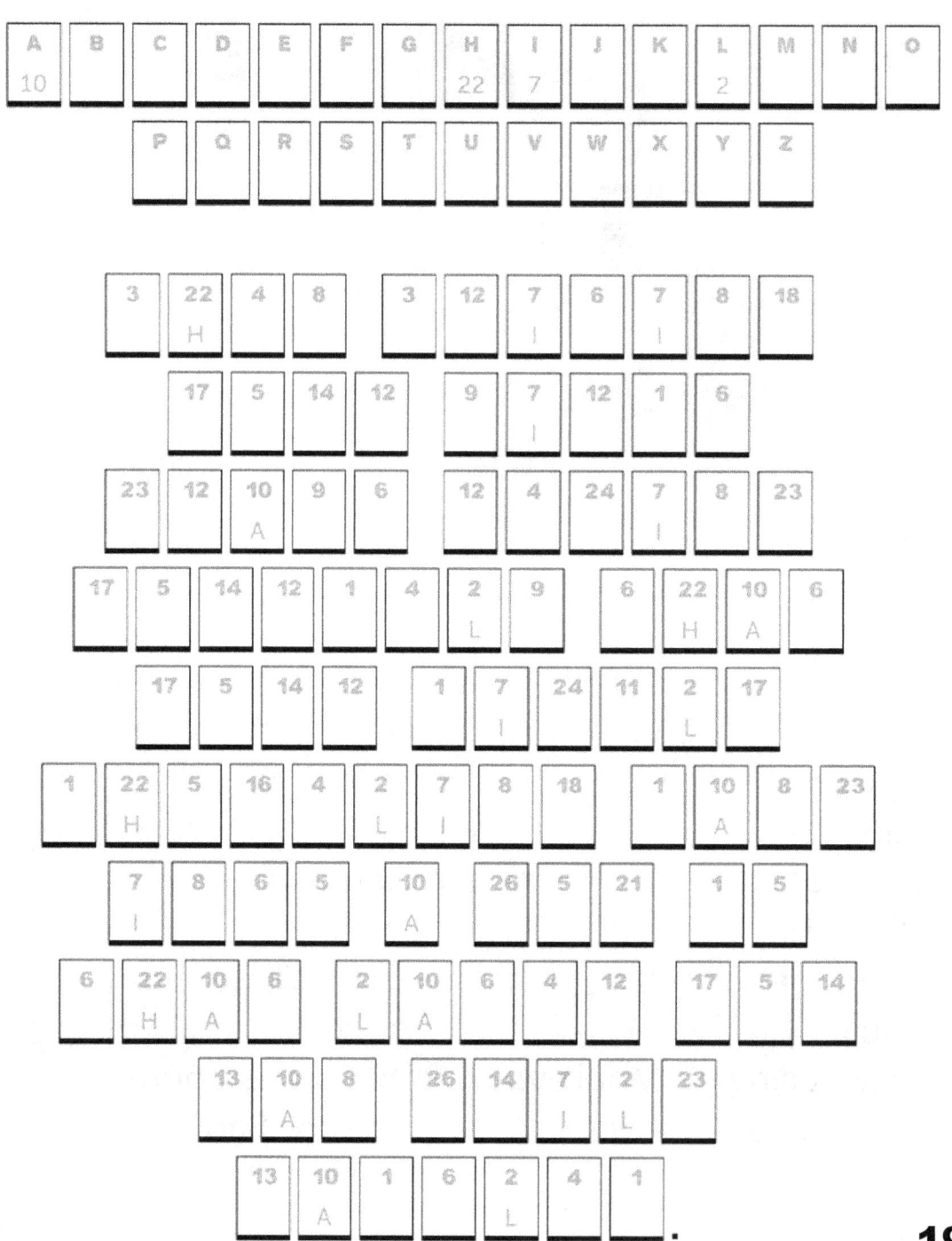

194

Christopher Rock

Christopher Rock

February 7, 1965 – PRESENT
COMEDIAN / ACTOR

195

LEFT BLANK ON PURPOSE

Christopher Rock

Christopher Rock

Christopher Rock

Christopher Rock

Christopher Rock

Christopher Rock

Directions: read the bio below and answer the following questions.

Hi, my name is Christopher Rock. I was born on February 7, 1965, in Andrews, SC. I attended James Madison High School. Although I dropped out, I later got my General Educational Development (GED) diploma. I started my career at a chain of comedy clubs called Catch a Rising Star in New York, where I performed standup. Eddie Murphy noticed me and started mentoring me. In 1985, I made my film debut in Krush Groove as an extra. Eddie gave me my first role in Beverly Hills Cop II as the Playboy Mansion Valet in 1987. In 1987, I made my TV debut as Carson in Miami Vice. In 1990, I joined Saturday Night Live, where I worked for a few years. I also acted in a few episodes of In Living Color, which was one of the most popular comedy TV shows at the time. Some of the other films and TV shows that I have acted in are The Fresh Prince of Bel-Air, I'm Gonna Git You Sucka, The Moxy Show, New Jack City and Martin. In 1997, I made my creator, writer and executive producer debut with my show The Chris Rock Show.

1. What was the name of circuit I started doing comedy?
    A. The Apollo
    B. Catch a Rising Star
    C. Cotton Club
2. What year did I get my first role in film?
    A. 1985
    B. 1987
    C. 1990
3. I wrote produced and created which show?
    A. I'm Gonna Git You Sucka
    B. The Chris Rock Show
    C. Martin

Directions: Answer the questions, to solve the crossword puzzle. You can use the internet if you get stuck on any question.

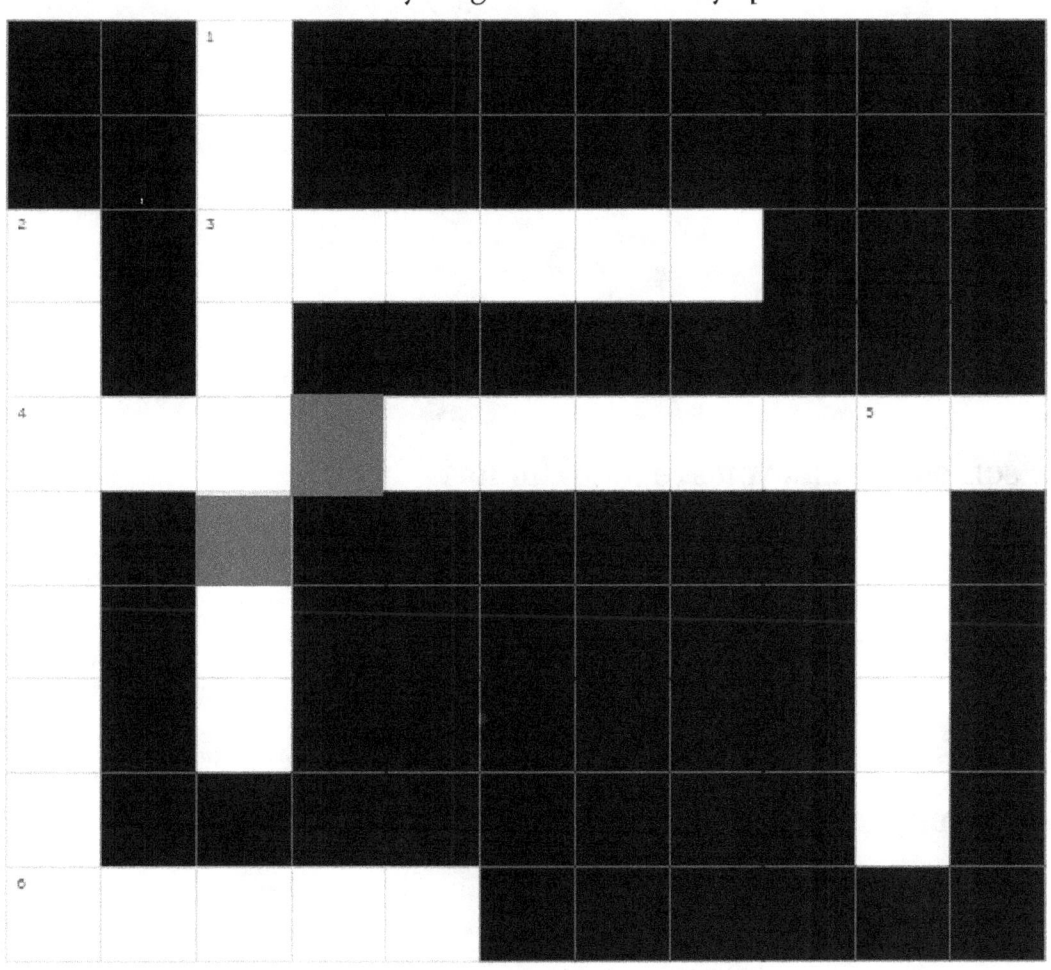

Across
3) Chris is the ___ of the best-selling book, 'Rock This'.
4) Chris had jobs as a hospital orderly and busboy at a ___.
6) Chris made his film ___ in Eddie Murphy's film Beverly Hills Cop II.

Down
1) Chris ranked number five on Comedy Central's and Rolling Stone 's list of Best ___ Comics of All Time.
2) Chris co-created, executive-produced and ___ his show "Everybody Hates Chris."
5) Chris won his first two __ for his 1996 HBO special, Chris Rock: Bring the Pain.

199

Directions: Read and answer the questions. These are your opinions so the answers will vary.

If you could meet one celebrity, who would it be?

What is something that you are thankful for?

What is a family tradition that you have?

Directions: Unscramble the words below about Chris. See if you can get the bonus word.

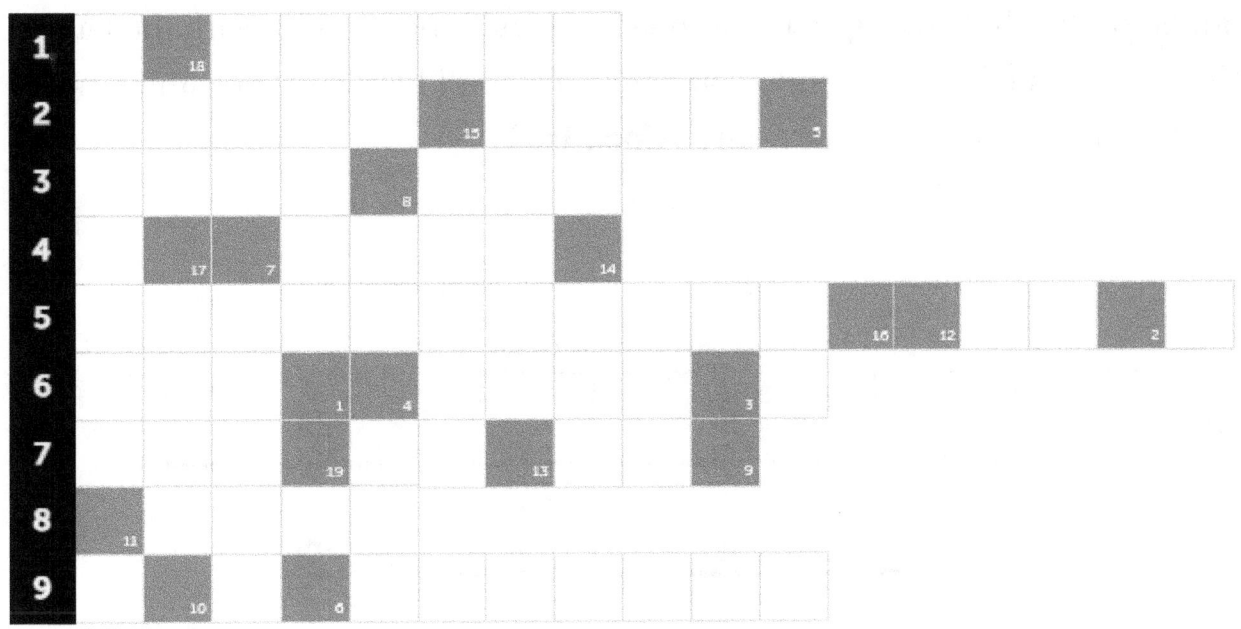

BONUS WORD

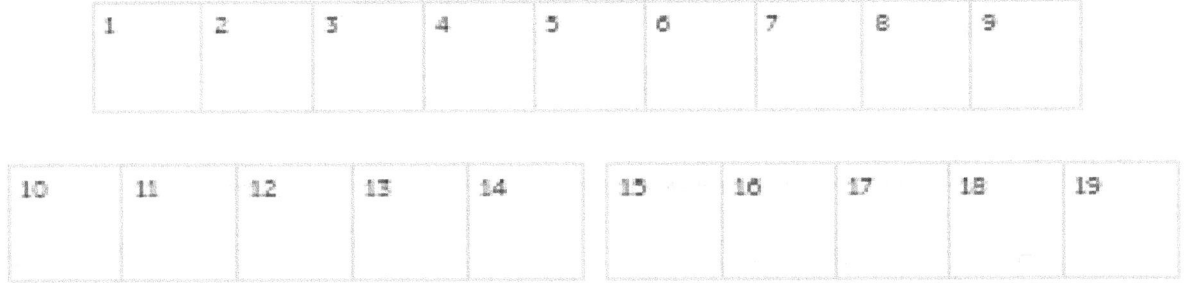

Unscramble Words

1) klaemfri
2) tcyjaiecknw
3) dmcoaien
4) osuwgrpn
5) htatigvsladuryeni
6) drervaecsen
7) srunettybe
8) racto
9) iehetobvmee

Directions: This is the WGLT Challenge. Solve the cryptogram. As the puzzle solver, you need to find which number belongs to which character. And this can be pretty challenging! You will need to match the number with the letter. There are some letters given to you below. This will help you solve the other words and unlock more characters. **Good Luck.**

1. Where did I perform when I started?
   A. Vaudeville-style minstrel show
   B. The Pearl Bailey Show
   C. The Bill Cosby show
2. What year did I perform at the Carnegie Hall?
   A. 1960
   B. 1961
   C. 1962
3. What name did I acquire as I kept performing?
   A. Jackie Mabley
   B. Jackie "Moms" Mabley
   C. Jackie

Loretta Mary Aiken
Answers

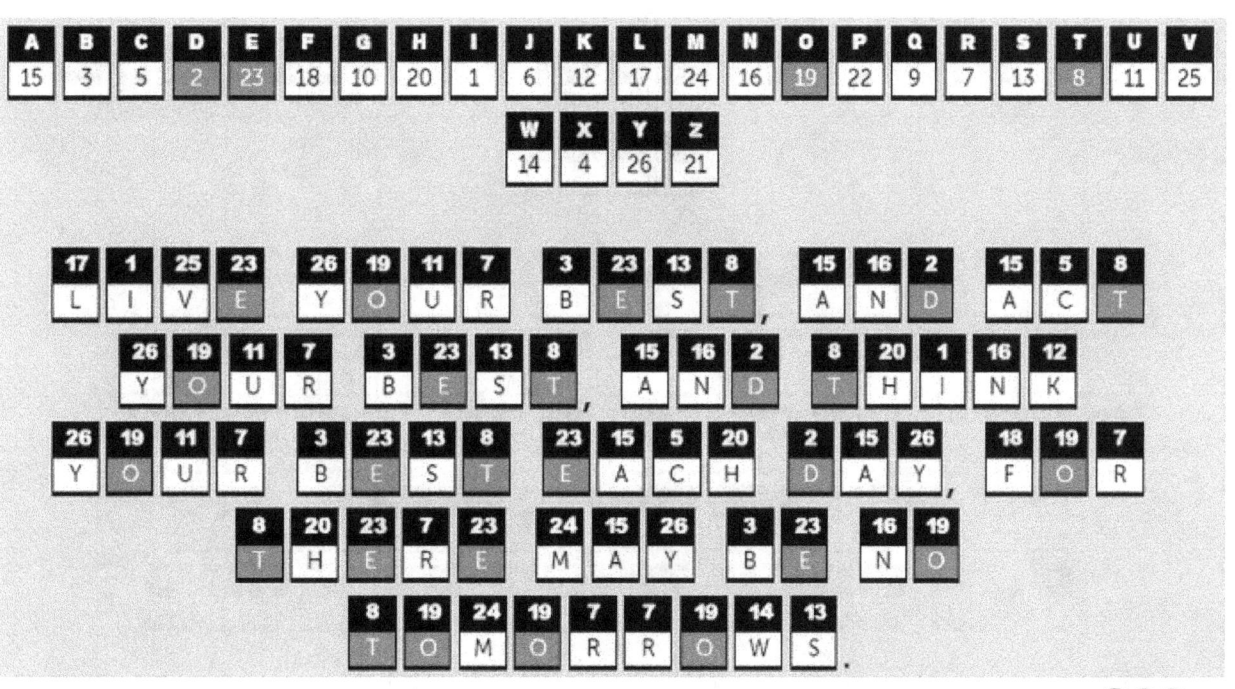

LIVE YOUR BEST, AND ACT YOUR BEST, AND THINK YOUR BEST EACH DAY, FOR THERE MAY BE NO TOMORROWS.

203

Bernard Jeffrey McCullough
Answers

1. What was the name of my High School?
   A. Jesuit High School
   B. Lindblom Math & Science Academy High School
   C. Chicago Vocational High School
2. What year did I start doing comedy?
   A. 1979
   B. 1977
   C. 1999
3. I made my breakthrough doing what show?
   A. HBO's Def Comedy Jam
   B. The Apollo
   C. Chicago Regal Theatre

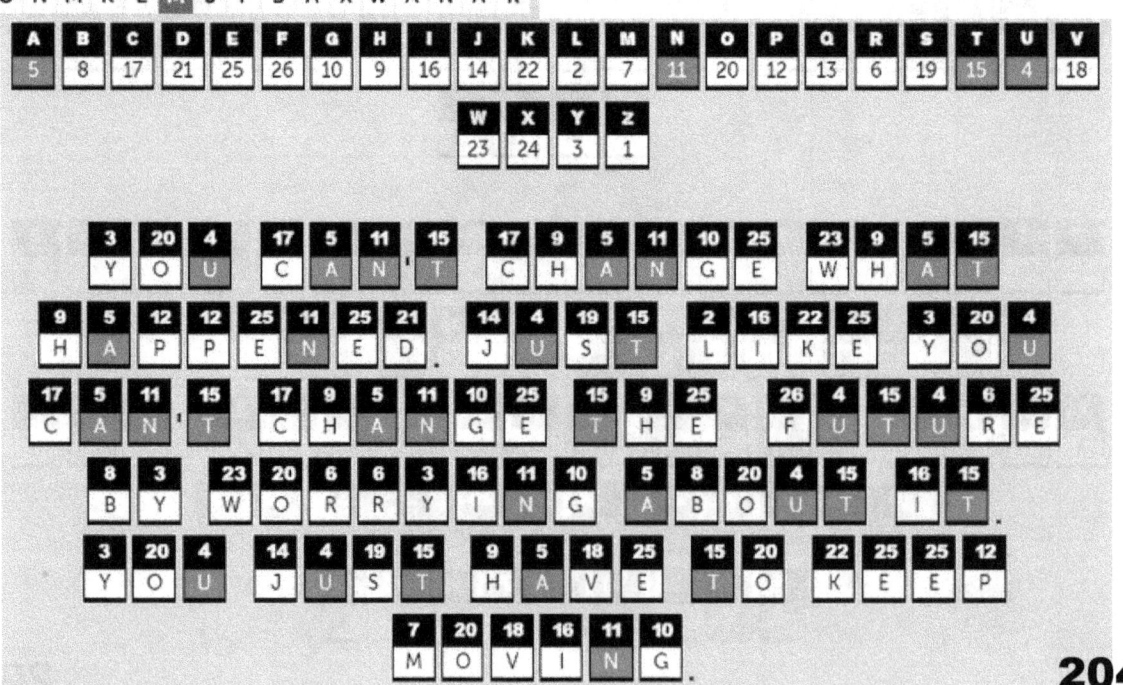

"You can't change what happened. Just like you can't change the future by worrying about it. You just have to keep moving."

204

1. What is the name of my sorority?
   A. Delta Gamma Theta
   B. Sigma Gamma Rho
   C. Alpha Kappa Alpha
2. What HBCU did I go to?
   A. Spellman College
   B. Hampton University
   C. Fisk University
3. What show did I get to write for and play a role in?
   A. The Keenen Ivory Wayans Show
   B. Will & Grace
   C. The Chris Rock Show

Wanda Yvette Sykes
Answers

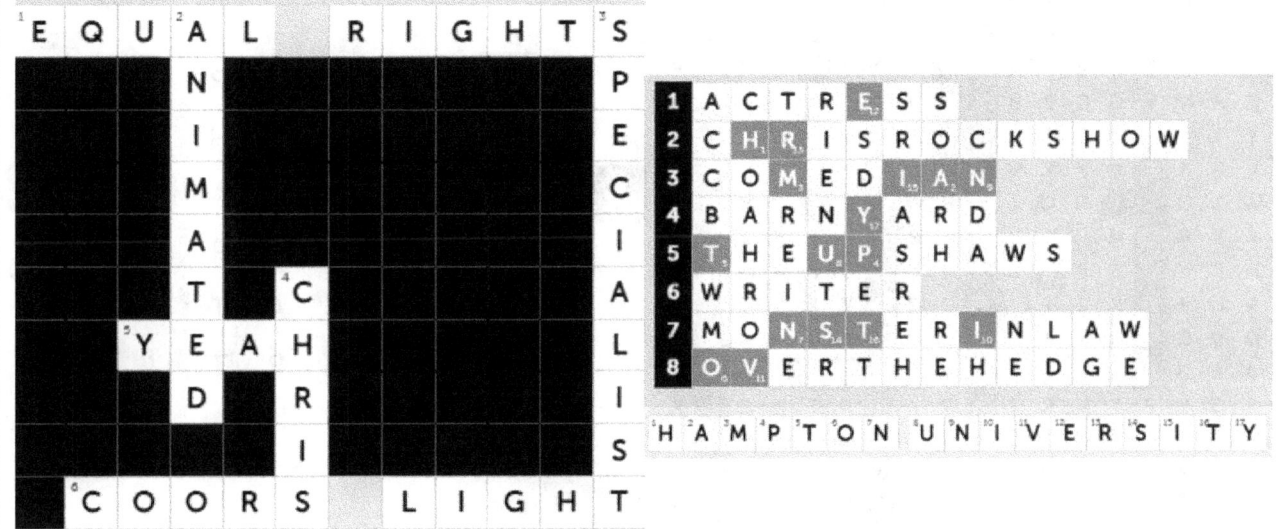

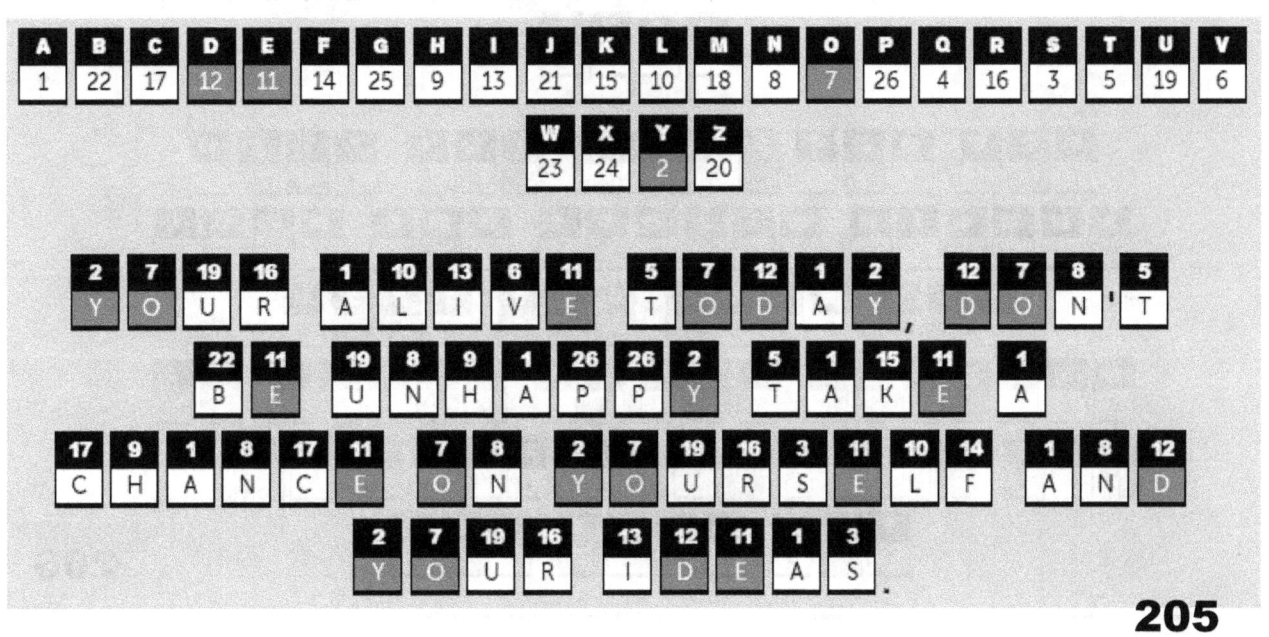

YOUR ALIVE TODAY, DON'T BE UNHAPPY TAKE A CHANCE ON YOURSELF AND YOUR IDEAS.

1. Who did I imitate in my youth talent show?
   A. Richard Pryor
   B. Al Greene
   C. Redd Foxx
2. What year did I start working at SNL?
   A. 1984
   B. 1982
   C. 1980
3. Which movie did I star in help write and produce?
   A. Life
   B. Mulan
   C. Daddy Day Care

Edward Regan Murphy

Answers

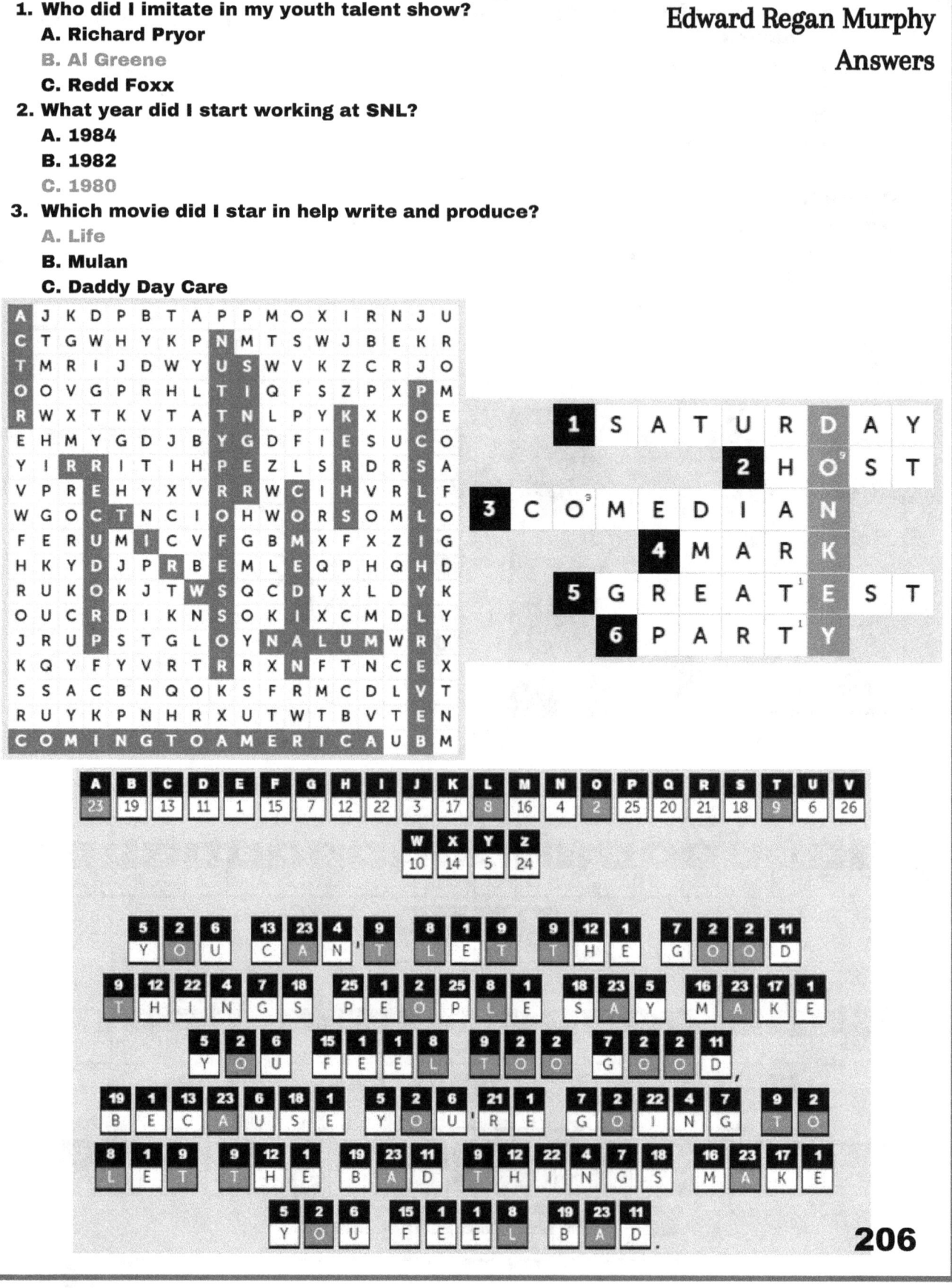

206

1. Where did I get my stage name from?
   A. My Mom
   B. The phrase whoopee cushion
   C. My acting teacher
2. I'm the first black woman to have achieved what?
   A. To win Academy Award for Best Supporting Actress
   B. To achieve EGOT status
   C. To win Academy Award for Best Actress
3. I became the first black woman to host?
   A. The Academy Awards
   B. Good Morning America
   C. The Golden Globe Awards

Caryn Elaine Johnson

Answers

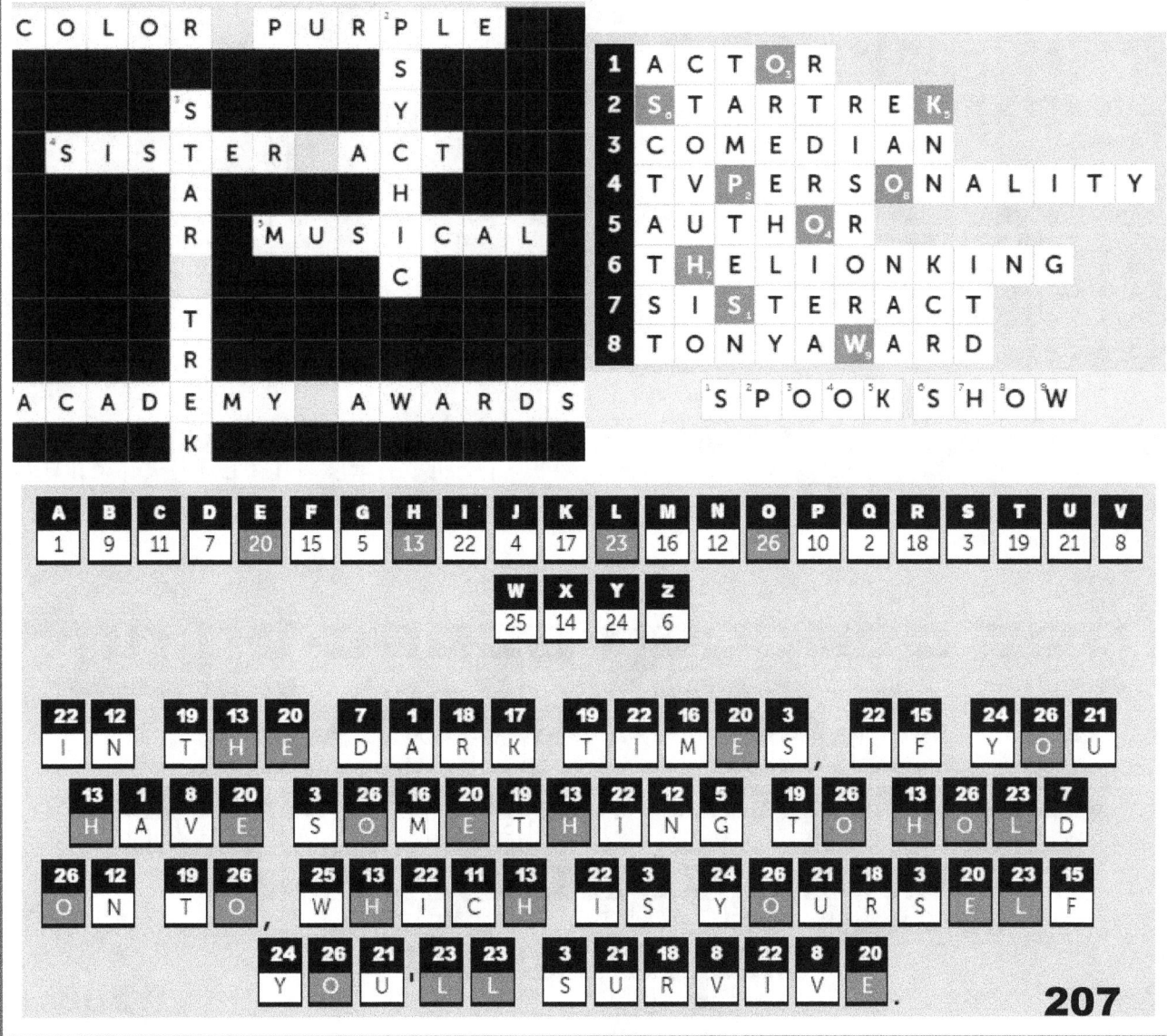

IN THE DARK TIMES, IF YOU HAVE SOMETHING TO HOLD ONTO, WHICH IS YOURSELF YOU'LL SURVIVE.

207

1. What was the name of the High School I graduate from?
   A. Eastern High School
   B. Anacostia High School
   C. Duke Ellington School of the Arts
2. What show did I start getting film and tv recognition?
   A. Def Comedy Jam
   B. Star Search
   C. Apollo Theater
3. What show did I co-write and star in?
   A. The Nutty Professor
   B. Half Baked
   C. Undercover Brother

David Chappelle

Answers

Crossword:
1. ROBIN
2. AMATEUR
3. HALF-BAKED
4. STAND-UP
5. NINETEEN
6. EMMY
7. BEST

Cryptogram:
THE HARDEST THING TO DO IS TO BE TRUE TO YOURSELF, ESPECIALLY WHEN EVERYBODY IS WATCHING.

208

Alberta Peal Answers

1. What wasn't my nickname while I was fire dancing?
   A. The Bronze Goddess of Fire
   B. The Black Queen of Comedy
   C. LaWanda, the Flame Goddess
2. What year did I start working in TV?
   A. 1972
   B. 1971
   C. 1973
3. I'm best known as which character?
   A. The Bronze Goddess of Fire
   B. Aunt Esther
   C. The Black Queen of Comedy

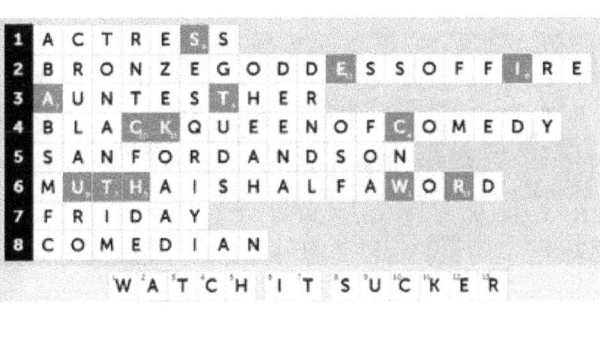
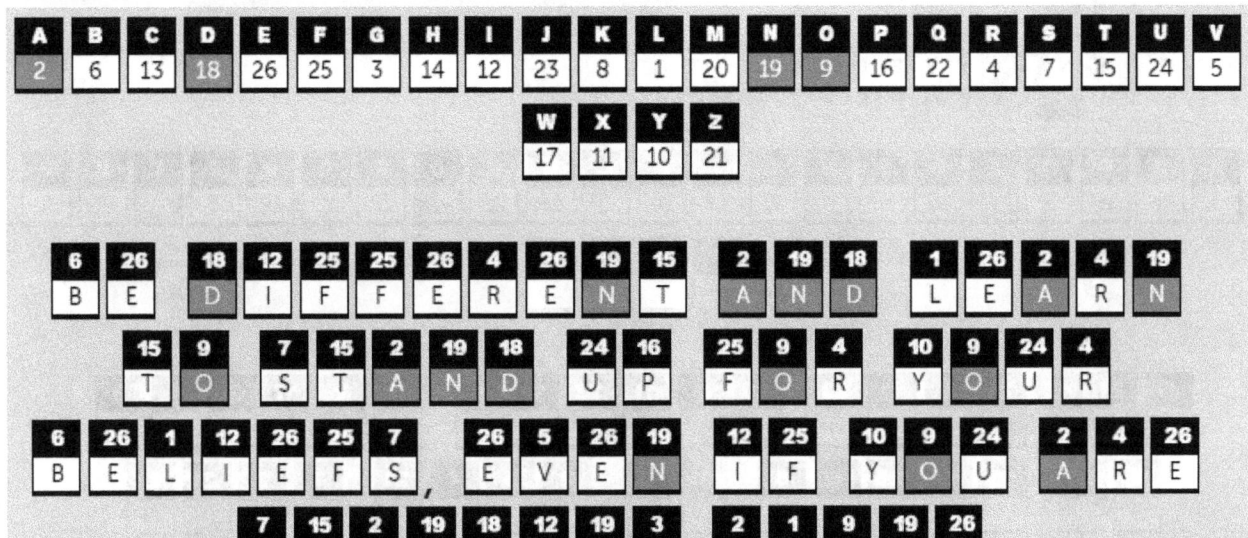

209

John Elroy Sanford
Answers

1. Who inspired me for my stage name?
   A. Chad Fox
   B. Jake Fox
   C. Jimmie Foxx
2. What year did I start acting in film?
   A. 1960
   B. 1955
   C. 1965
3. What was the name of my first show on TV?
   A. The Redd Foxx Comedy Hour
   B. Sandford and Son
   C. Sandford

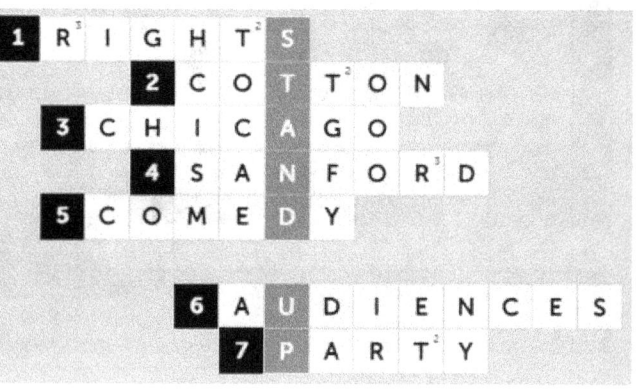

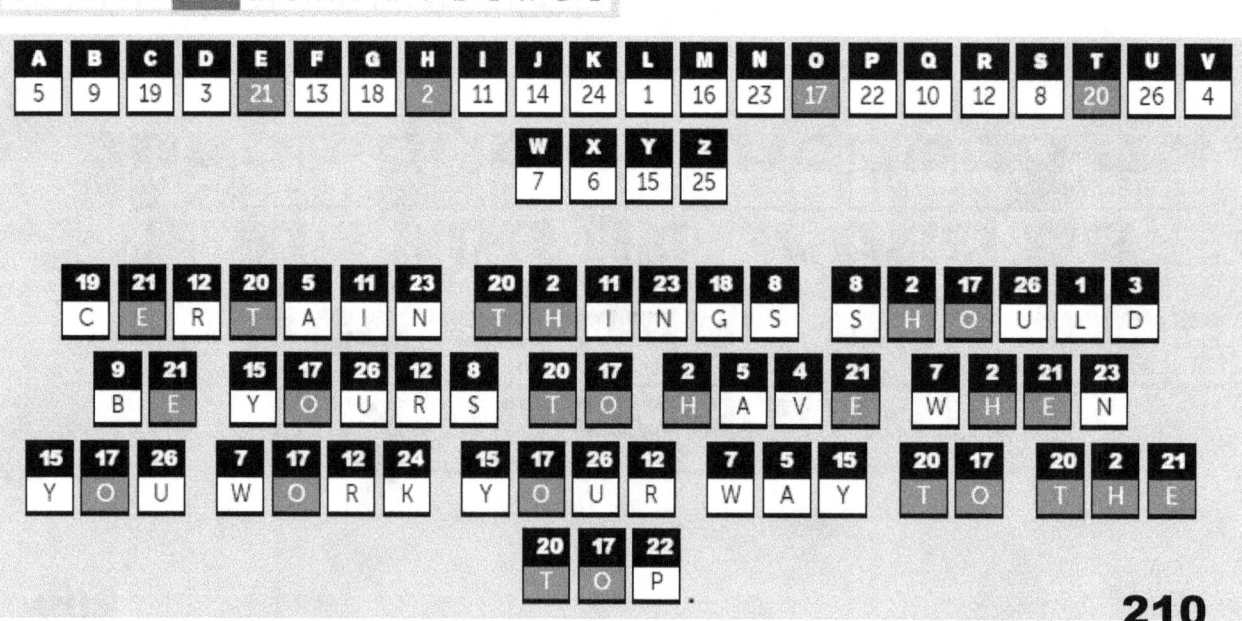

"CERTAIN THINGS SHOULD BE YOURS TO HAVE WHEN YOU WORK YOUR WAY TO THE TOP."

210

1. **What was the name of college I got my degree from?**
   A. Governor's State University
   B. Fresno City College
   C. University of Chicago
2. **What sorority do I belong to?**
   A. Alpha Kappa Alpha
   B. Zeta Phi Beta
   C. Delta Sigma Theta
3. **I won what award from BET?**
   A. Funniest Female Comedian on Comic View
   B. Best Actress
   C. Best Supporting Actress

Sheryl Underwood
Answers

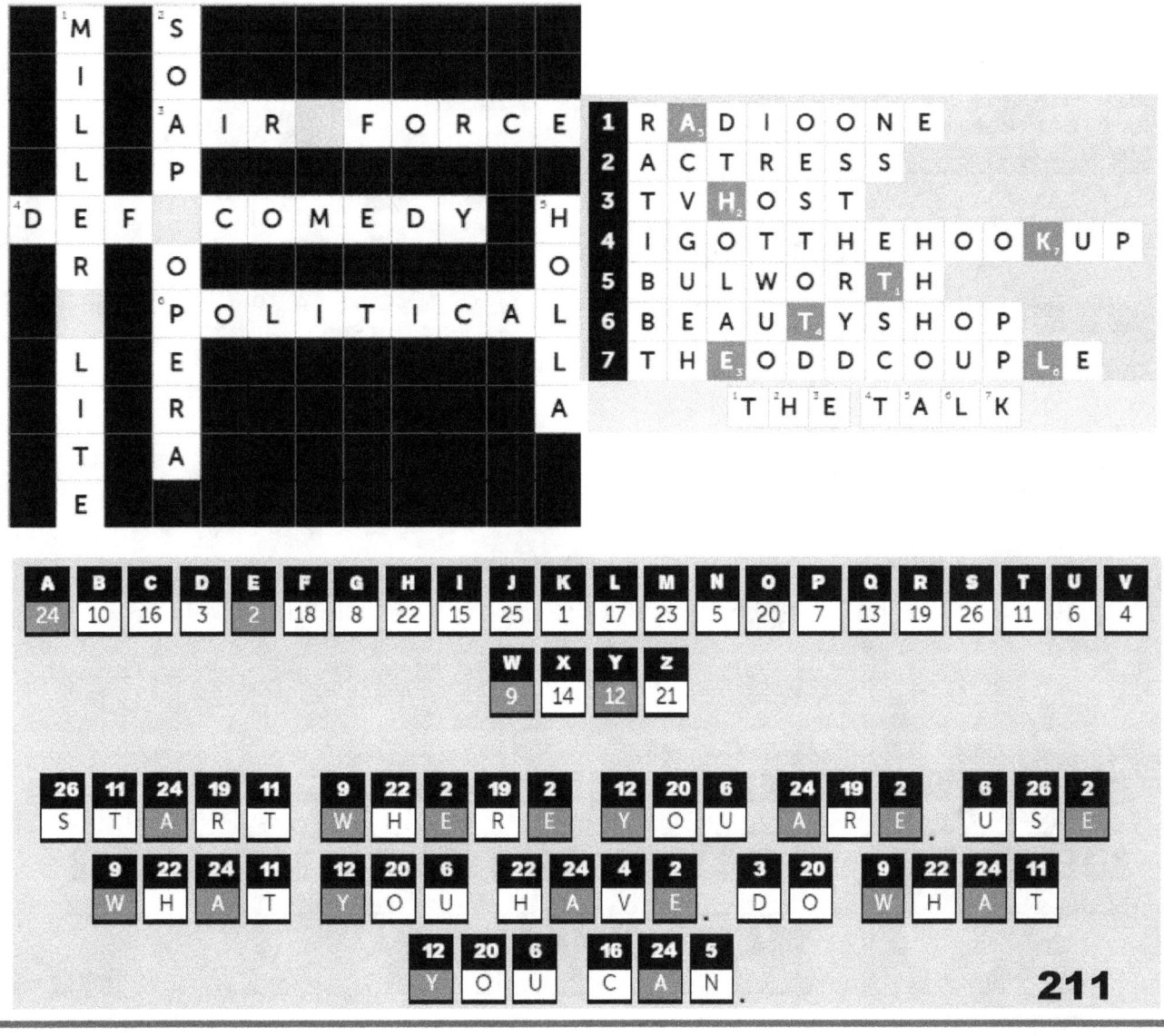

211

1. What was the branch of service that I served in?
   A. Navy
   B. Army
   C. Marine Corps
2. What year did I start doing comedy?
   A. 1954
   B. 1961
   C. 1958
3. I once ran for what branch of the U.S. government?
   A. Legislative
   B. Judicial
   C. Executive

Richard Gregory
Answers

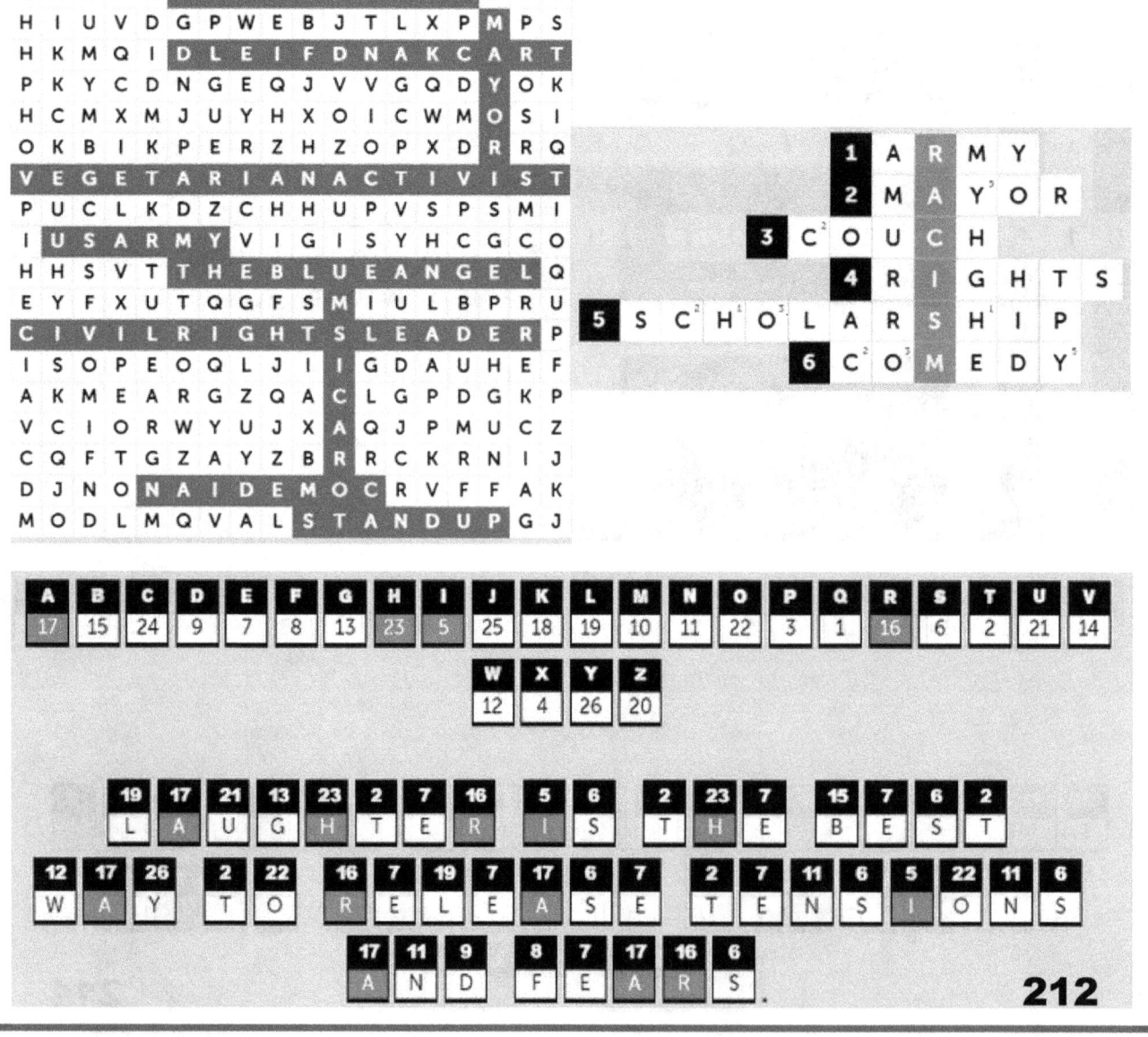

1. What was the name of my High School?
   A. Charles Evans Hughes High School
   B. Austin High School
   C. Morris High School
2. What year did I start acting?
   A. 1982
   B. 1975
   C. 1978
3. Which film did I Direct but not star in?
   A. Hollywood Shuffle
   B. The Five Heartbeats
   C. Black Lightning

Robert Townsend
Answers

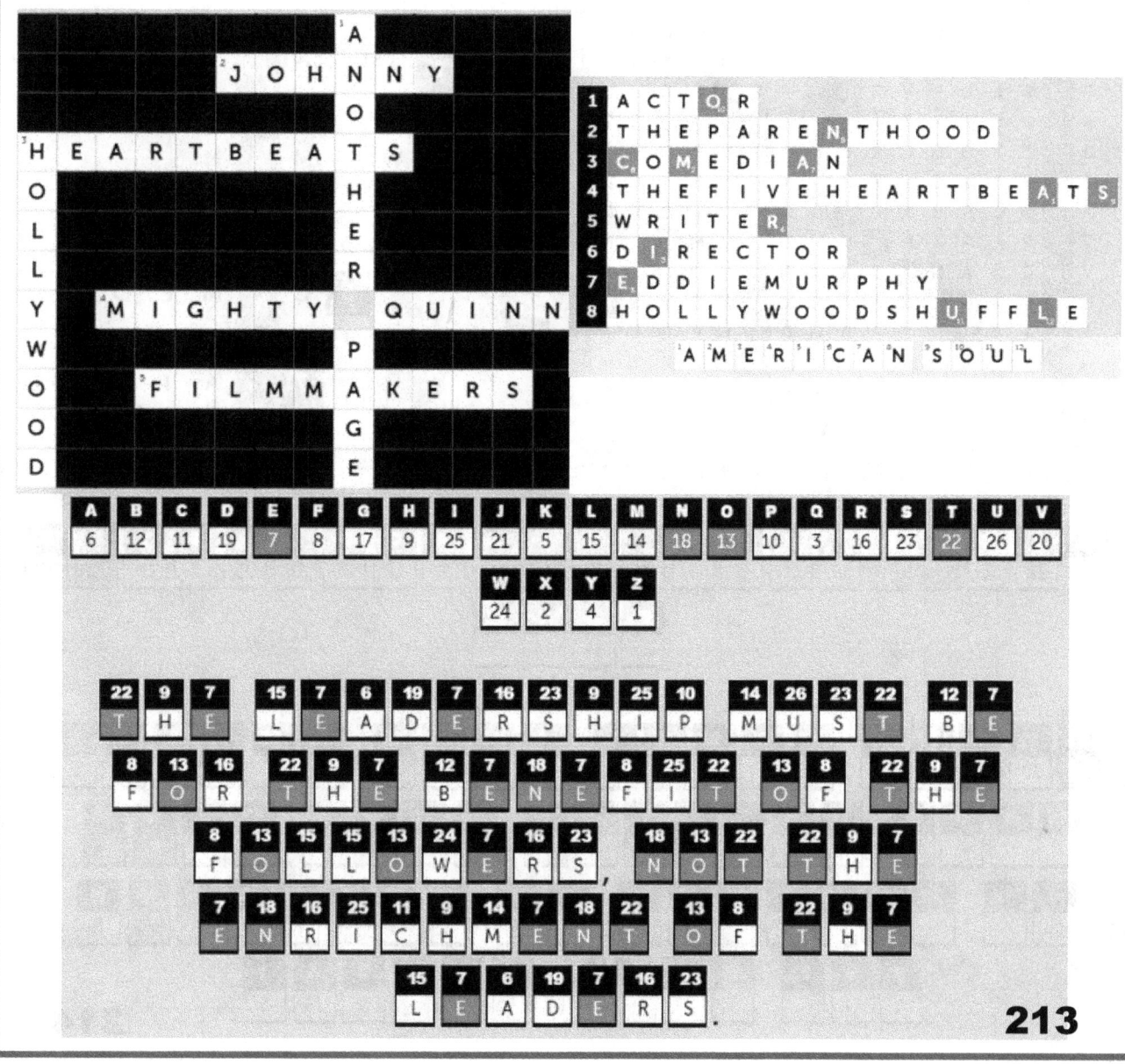

THE LEADERSHIP MUST BE FOR THE BENEFIT OF THE FOLLOWERS, NOT THE ENRICHMENT OF THE LEADERS.

213

1. What was the name of the HBCU I went to?
   A. Spellman College
   B. Morris Brown College
   C. Howard University
2. What year did I debut in TV?
   A. 1995
   B. 1996
   C. 1994
3. I set what Guinness Book of World Records?
   A. Performing for more than 75,000 people
   B. Performing for more than 50,000 people
   C. Performing for more than 60,000 people

Lori Rambough.
Answers

1. ALONE
2. COMIC
3. WOMAN
4. APOLLO
5. COMEDY
6. NATIONALLY
7. GAINED

DOUBT KILLS MORE DREAMS THAN FAILURE EVER WILL. SO BELIEVE IN YOURSELF AND YOUR DREAMS.

214

Broderick Harvey Sr
Answers

1. What fraternity am I a member of?
   A. Omega Psi Phi
   B. Alpha Phi Alpha
   C. Kappa Alpha Psi
2. What year did I start doing comedy?
   A. 1990
   B. 1985
   C. 1993
3. What show of mine is in syndication through the U.S.?
   A. Showtime at the Apollo
   B. Kings of Comedy
   C. The Steve Harvey Morning Show

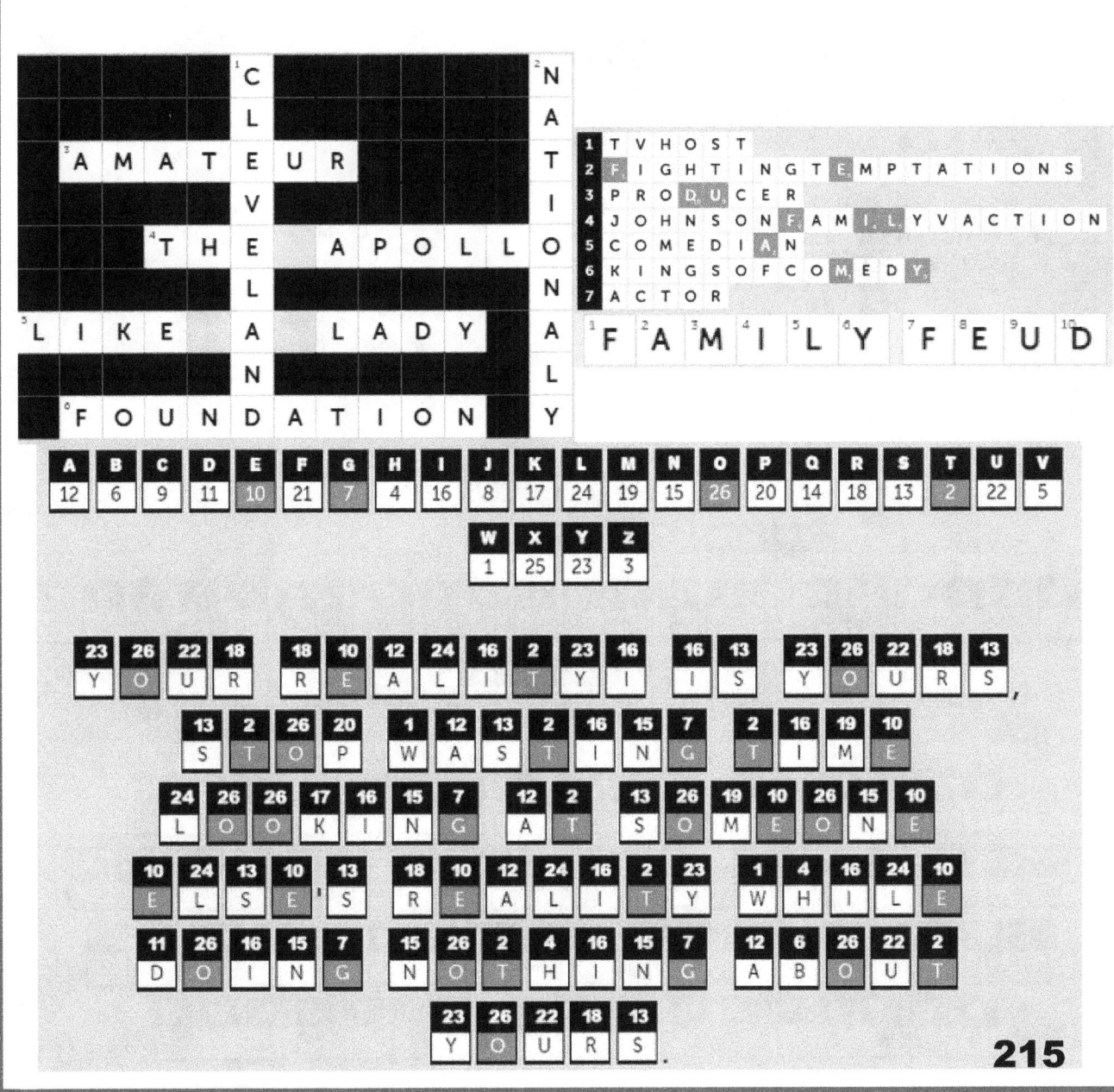

215

Broderick Smiley
Answers

1. What college did I get my Bachelors degree from?
   A. Tuskegee University
   B. Howard University
   C. Alabama State University
2. What fraternity do I belong to?
   A. Omega Psi Phi
   B. Kappa Alpha Psi
   C. Phi Beta Sigma
3. What award did I receive in 2004?
   A. Platinum Mic Viewer's Choice Award
   B. Network/Syndicated Personality of the Year
   C. Vision Award

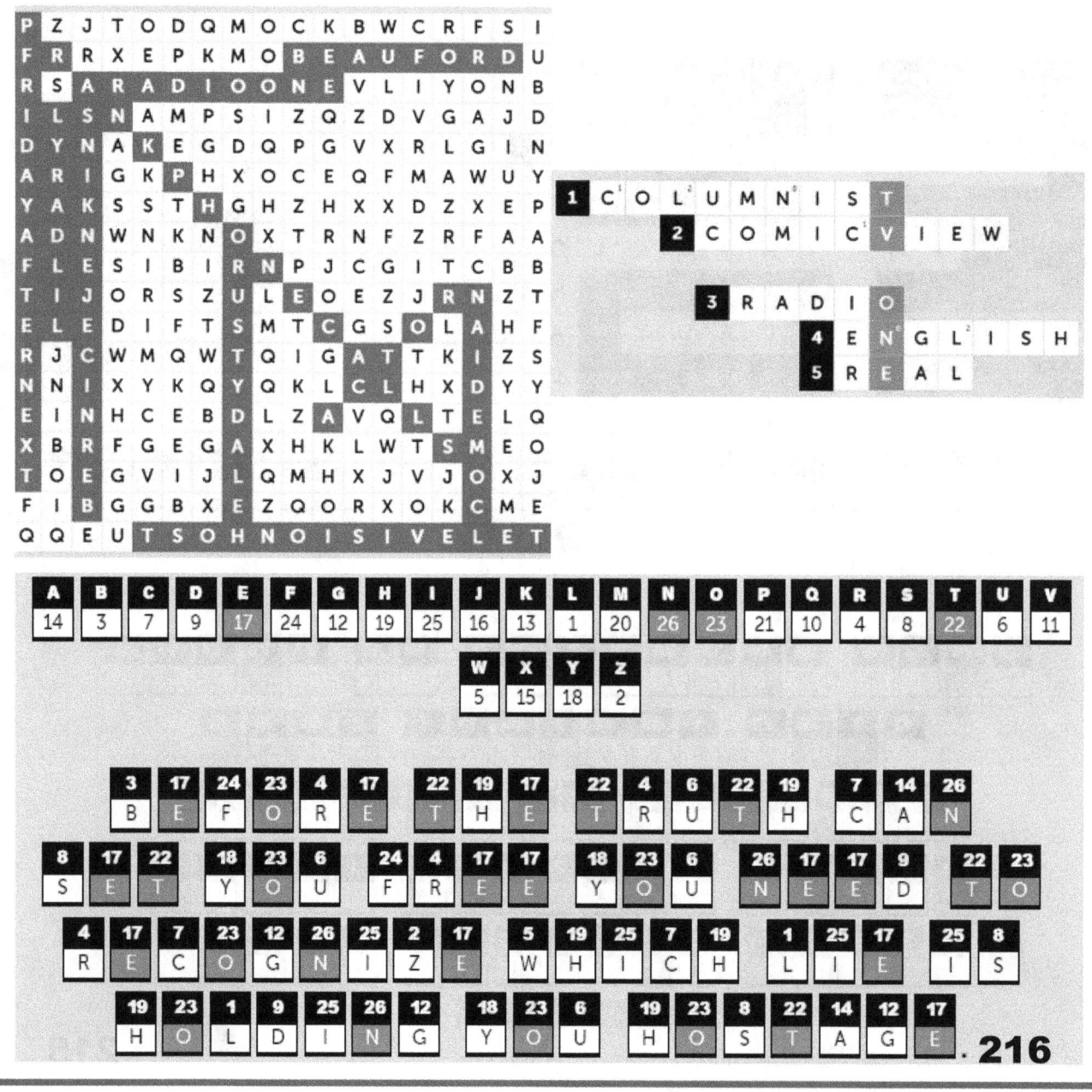

BEFORE THE TRUTH CAN SET YOU FREE YOU NEED TO RECOGNIZE WHICH LIE IS HOLDING YOU HOSTAGE

216

1. **What college did I graduate from?**
   A. Morgan State University
   B. University of Maryland
   C. The Broadcasting Institute of Maryland
2. **What year did I get my own show?**
   A. 1999
   B. 2000
   C. 2001
3. **I won this award unanimously?**
   A. Independent Spirit Award
   B. Academy Award for Best Supporting Actress
   C. AAFCA's Best Supporting Actress Award

Monique Hicks
Answers

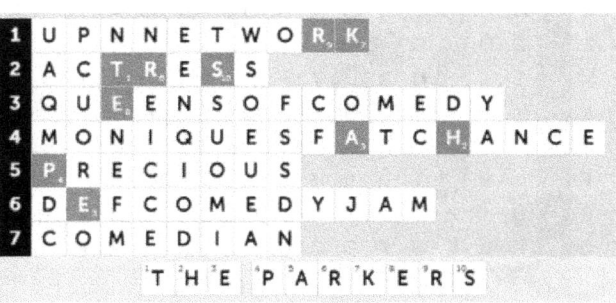

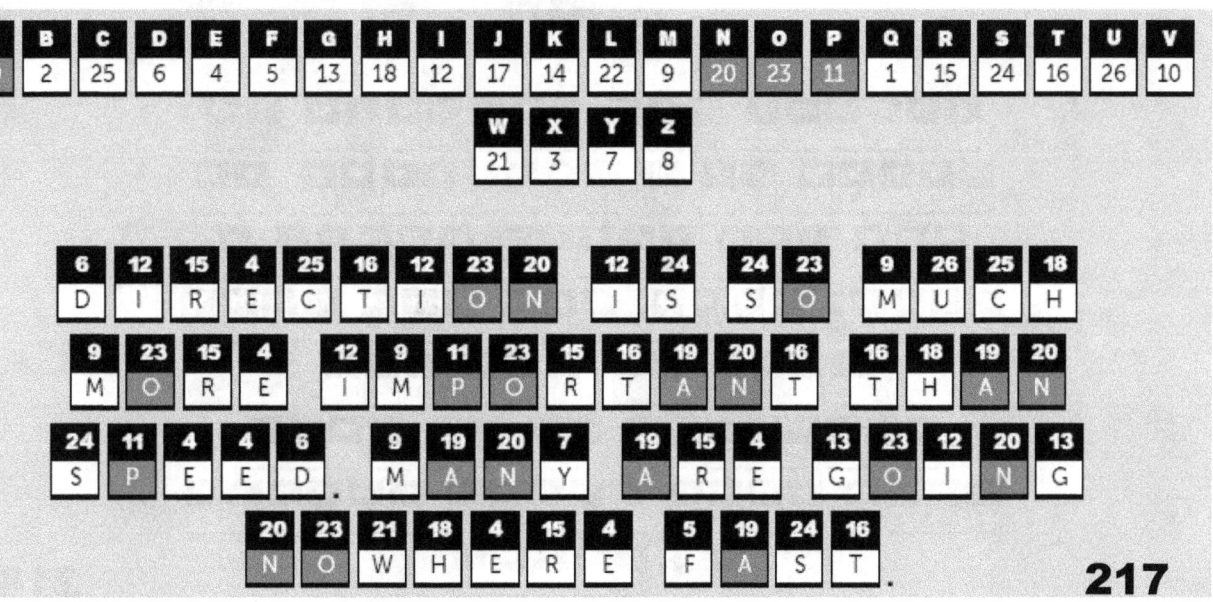

"DIRECTION IS SO MUCH MORE IMPORTANT THAN SPEED. MANY ARE GOING NOWHERE FAST."

1. **What branch of the service did I serve in?**
   A. Air Force
   B. Marine Corps
   C. Army
2. **I became the first black actor to?**
   A. Earn a million dollars for five films
   B. Earn a million dollars for a single film
   C. Earn a million dollars for two films
3. **I was the first person to win?**
   A. Oscar
   B. Mark Twain Prize for American Humor
   C. Golden Globe

Richard Pryor Sr

Answers

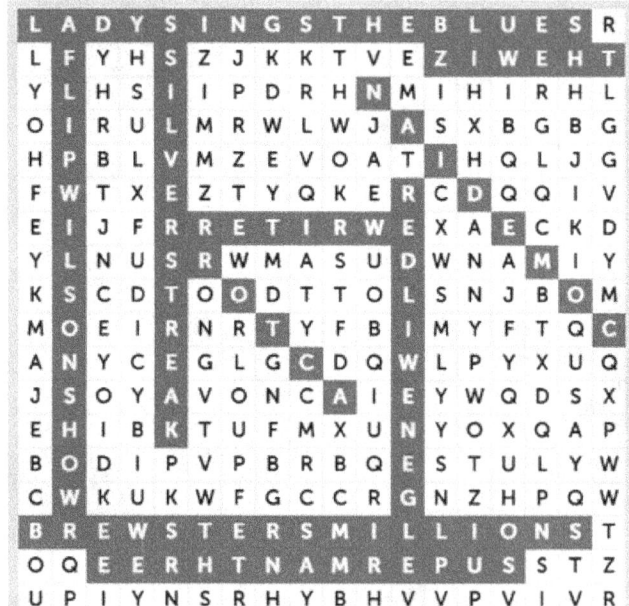

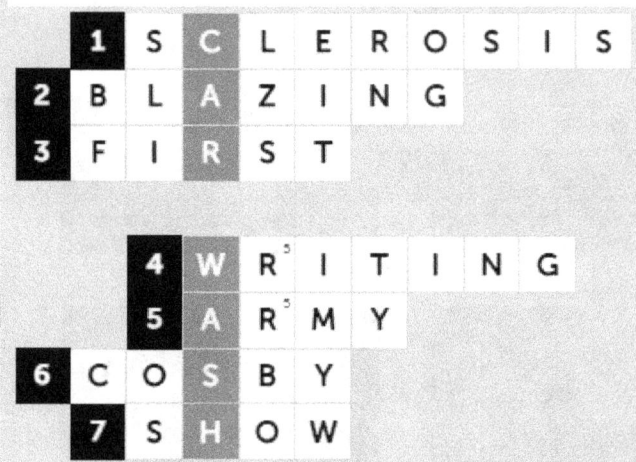

1. SCLEROSIS
2. BLAZING
3. FIRST
4. WRITING
5. ARMY
6. COSBY
7. SHOW

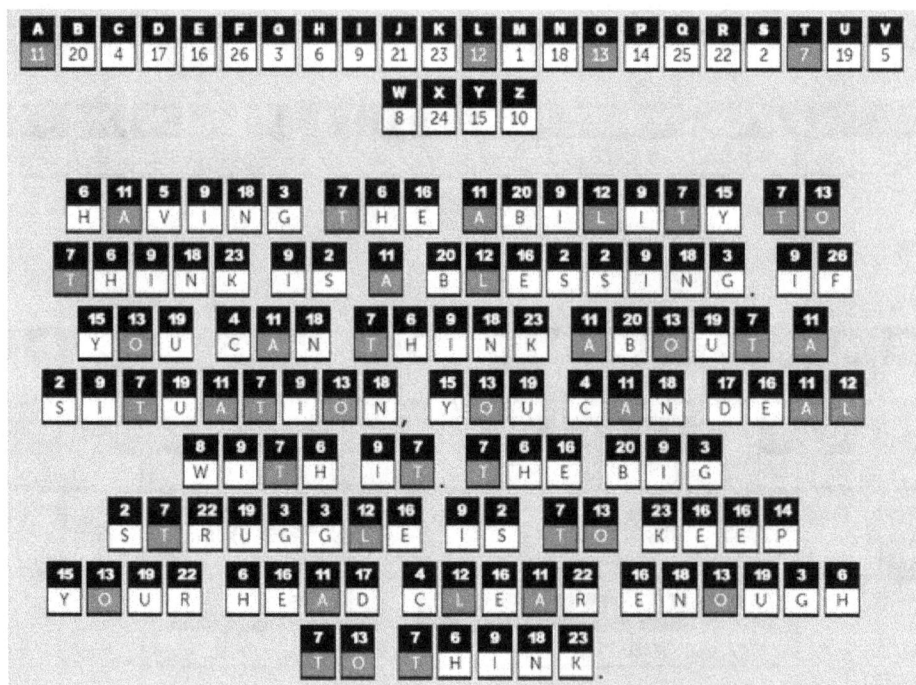

HAVING THE ABILITY TO THINK IS A BLESSING. IF YOU CAN THINK ABOUT A SITUATION, YOU CAN DEAL WITH IT. THE BIG STRUGGLE IS TO KEEP YOUR HEAD CLEAR ENOUGH TO THINK.

218

Cedric Antonio Kyles
Answers

1. What college did I get my Bachelors degree from?
   A. Missouri University
   B. Southeast Missouri State University
   C. Howard University
2. What year did I start doing films?
   A. 1987
   B. 1996
   C. 1998
3. Which film didn't I play in?
   A. Ice Age
   B. Madagascar
   C. The Proud Family

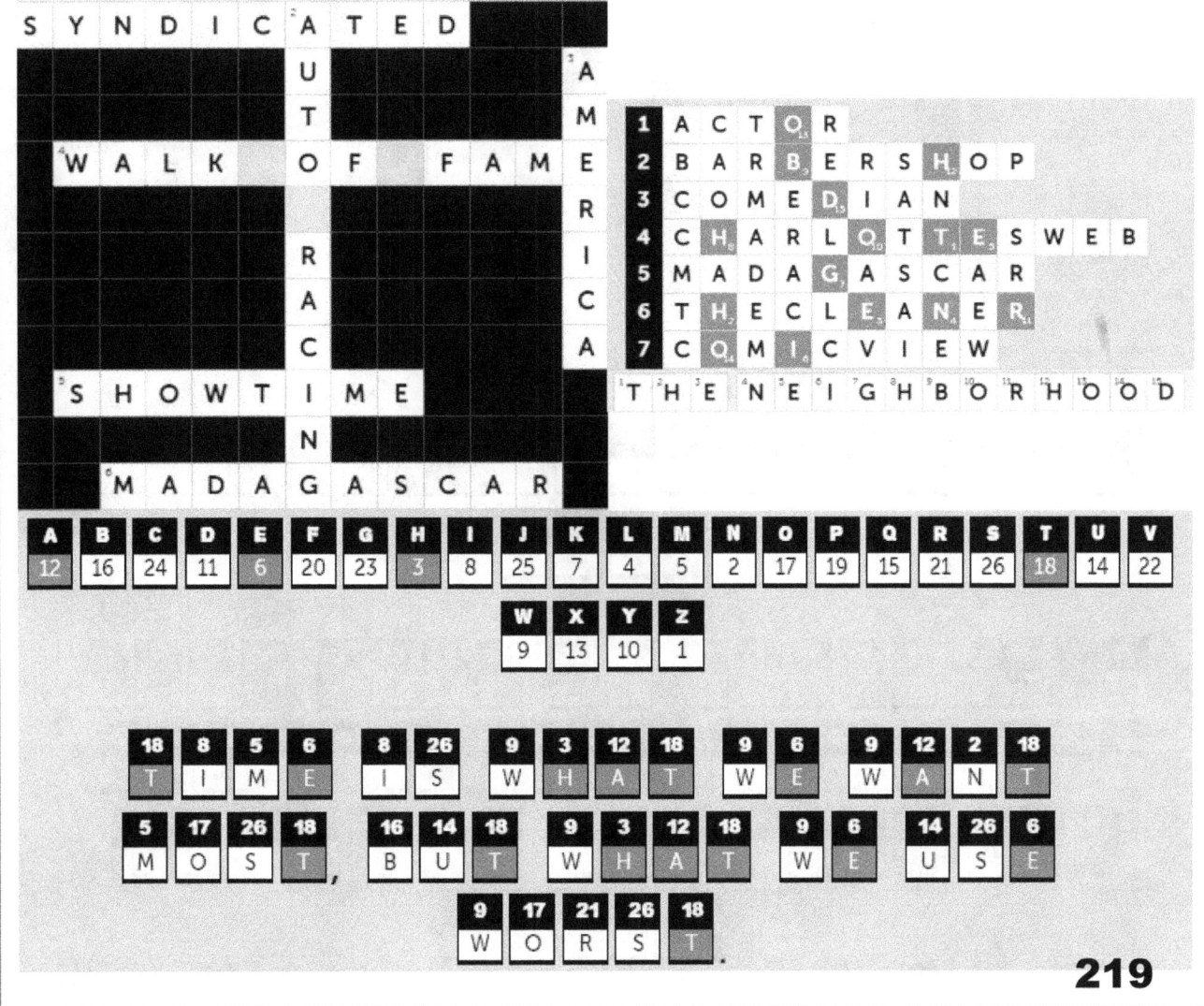

Tiffany Haddish Answers

1. What was the name of my High School?
   A. Charles Evans Hughes High School
   B. El Camino Real High School
   C. Morris High School
2. What year did I start my film debut?
   A. 2006
   B. 2005
   C. 2008
3. Which is not a film of mine?
   A. Bad Trip
   B. That's So Raven
   C. Girls Trip

220

Keenen Ivory Wayans
Answers

1. What HBCU did I attend?
   A. Howard University
   B. Tuskegee University
   C. Fisk University
2. What did I help produce but didn't play a role in?
   A. White Chicks
   B. Most Wanted
   C. Eddie Murphy Raw
3. I created which comedy show in the 90's?
   A. The Fresh Prince of Bel-Air
   B. Martin
   C. In Living Color

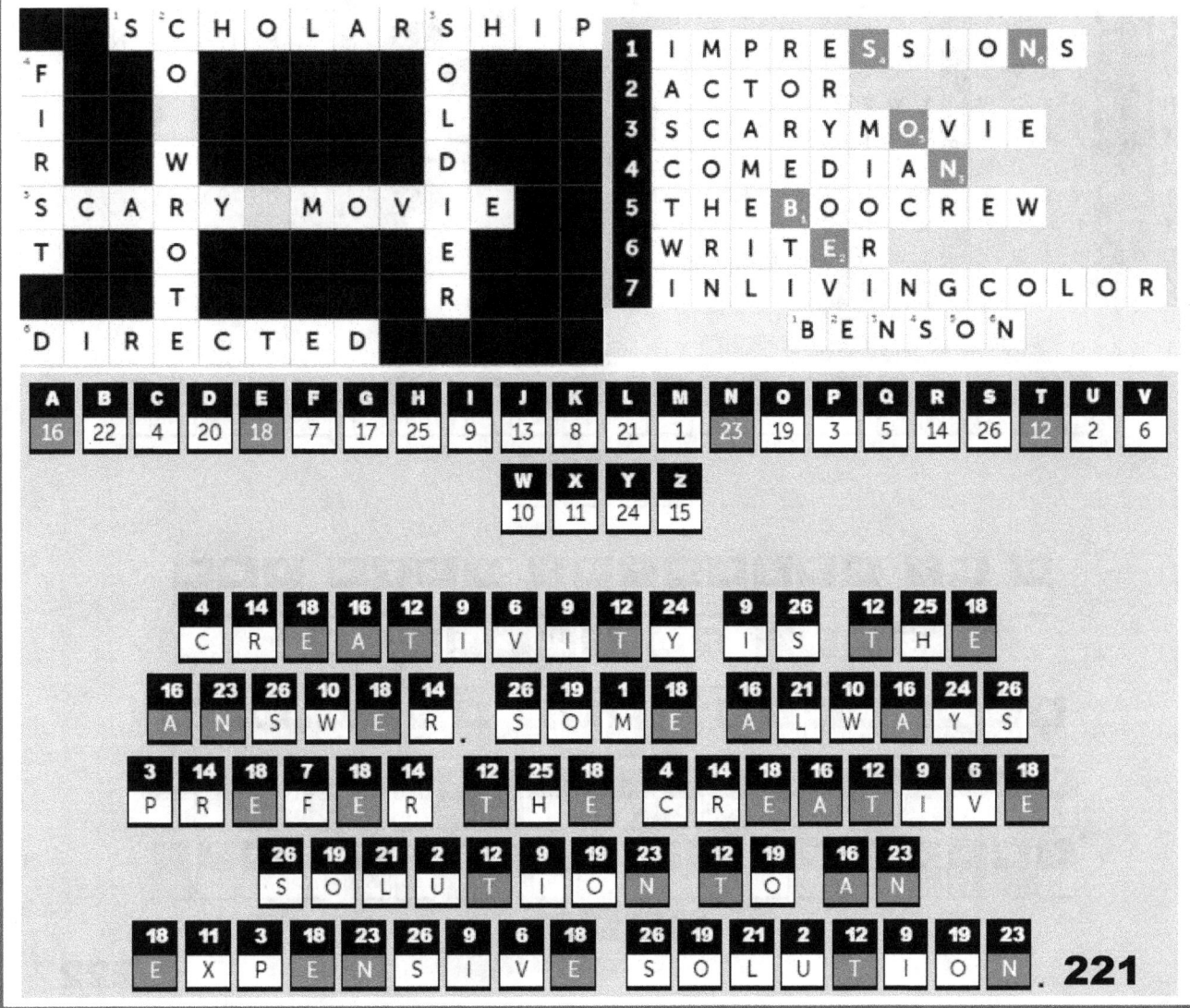

CREATIVITY IS THE ANSWER. SOME ALWAYS PREFER THE CREATIVE SOLUTION TO AN EXPENSIVE SOLUTION.

221

1. What college did I get my Bachelors degree from?
   A. Ohio University
   B. Kent State University
   C. Cleveland State University
2. What year did I get my own late night show?
   A. 1987
   B. 1989
   C. 1988
3. I was the first African-American to do what in the U.S.?
   A. Have my Own Company
   B. Have my Own Late Night Show
   C. Have my Own Day Time Show

Arsenio Hall
Answers

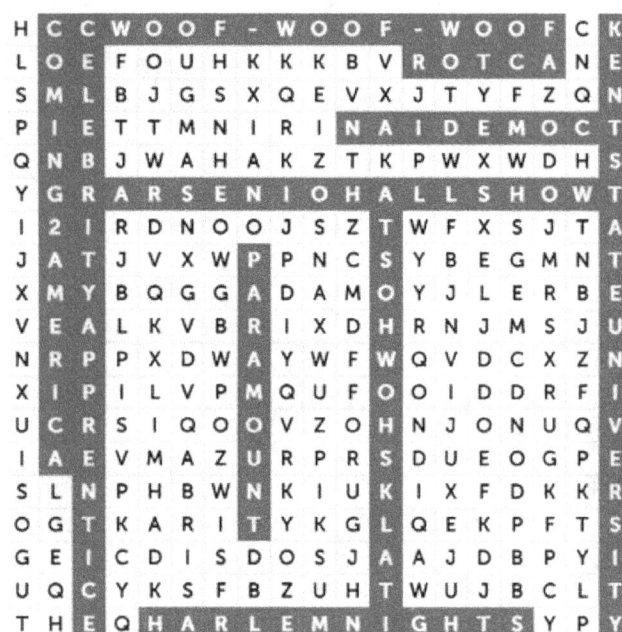

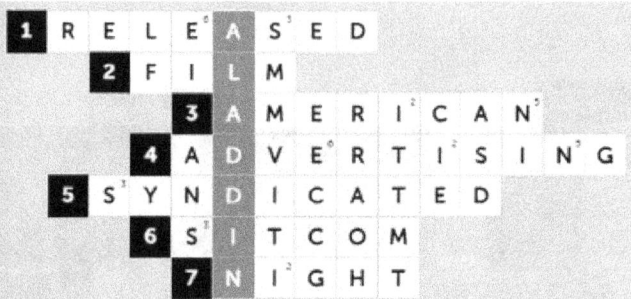

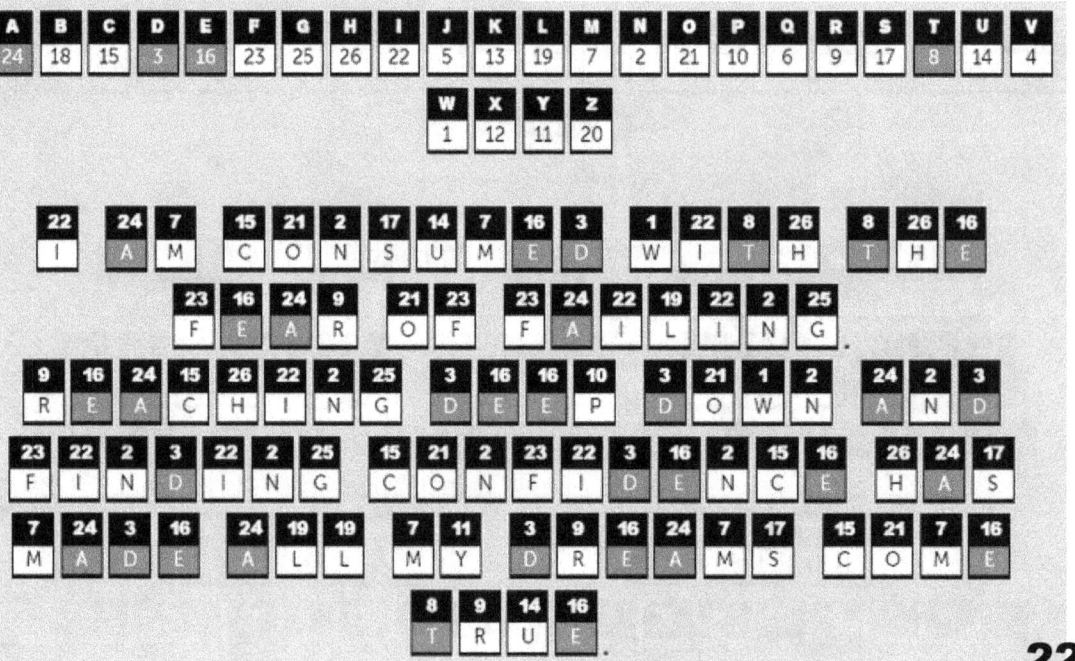

I AM CONSUMED WITH THE FEAR OF FAILING. REACHING DEEP DOWN AND FINDING CONFIDENCE HAS MADE ALL MY DREAMS COME TRUE.

222

1. What college didn't I go to?
   A. UCLA
   B. Colorado State University
   C. Chapman University
2. How did I start doing comedy?
   A. Comedy Open Mic
   B. Funniest Person on Campus" contest
   C. Dare from my Dad
3. I use to work on this show?
   A. Saturday Night Live
   B. Key & Peele
   C. Martin

Annette "Leslie" Jones

Answers

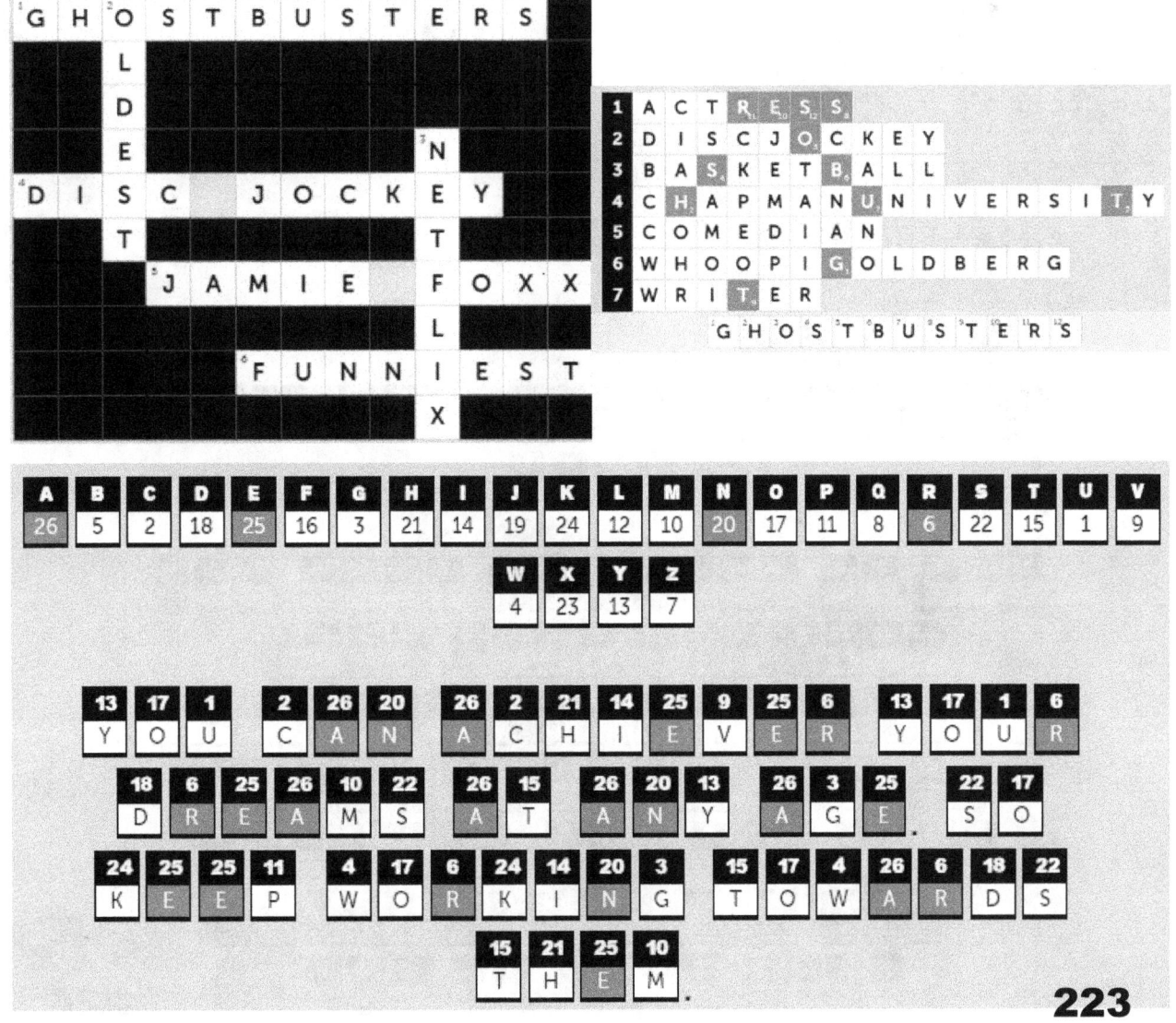

223

Martin Lawrence Answers

1. What did I do before I started comedy?
   A. Computer Programming
   B. Golden Gloves boxing
   C. Teacher
2. What year did I start doing films?
   A. 1987
   B. 1989
   C. 1990
3. Which show did I create and star in?
   A. Star Search
   B. Martin
   C. Def Comedy Jam

Word search contains: MARTIN, DIRECTOR, BAD BOYS 2, BIG MOMMAS HOUSE, ACTOR, COMEDIAN, etc.

Crossword:
1. BETWEEN
2. SEARCH
3. GOLDEN
4. LEBRON
5. NERVOUS
6. KENNEDY
7. SEARS

Cipher key:
A	B	C	D	E	F	G	H	I	J	K	L	M	N	O	P	Q	R	S	T	U	V
12	18	8	7	9	6	19	5	20	22	3	25	24	11	1	10	17	13	16	23	21	15

W	X	Y	Z
2	26	4	14

"TRY TO MAKE DUE WITH THE TIME YOU HAVE HERE. HOPEFULLY WHEN YOU PASS ON, SOMEBODY CAN LOOK BACK AND SAY, WOW THEY MADE A DIFFERENCE IN SOME KIND OF WAY."

224

1. **What was the name of my High School?**
   A. George Washington High School
   B. Barack Obama Green Charter High School
   C. John F. Kennedy High School
2. **What year did I start acting and TV?**
   A. 2000
   B. 2002
   C. 2004
3. **I founded what company in 2009?**
   A. Help From the Hart Charity (HFTH)
   B. Laugh Out Loud
   C. HartBeat Productions

Kevin Hart Answers

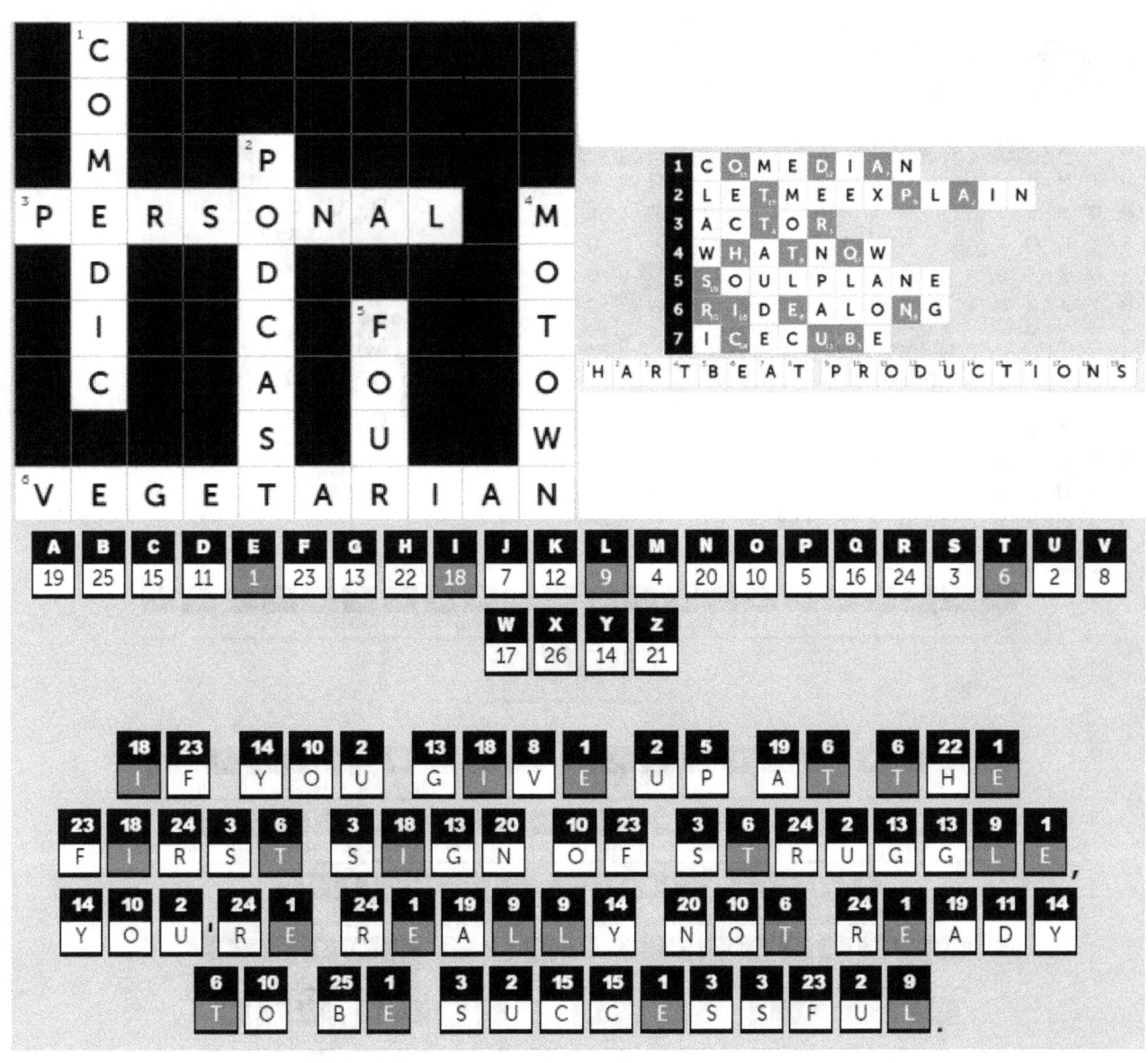

225

1. Where didn't I start out performing at?
   A. Boom Chicago
   B. The Second City
   C. Mad TV
2. What year did I start doing Directing?
   A. 2008
   B. 2017
   C. 2003
3. I was the first African-American screenwriter to win?
   A. Golden Globe for Best Original Screenplay
   B. Academy Award for Best Original Screenplay
   C. Emmy for Best Original Screenplay

Jordan Peele
Answers

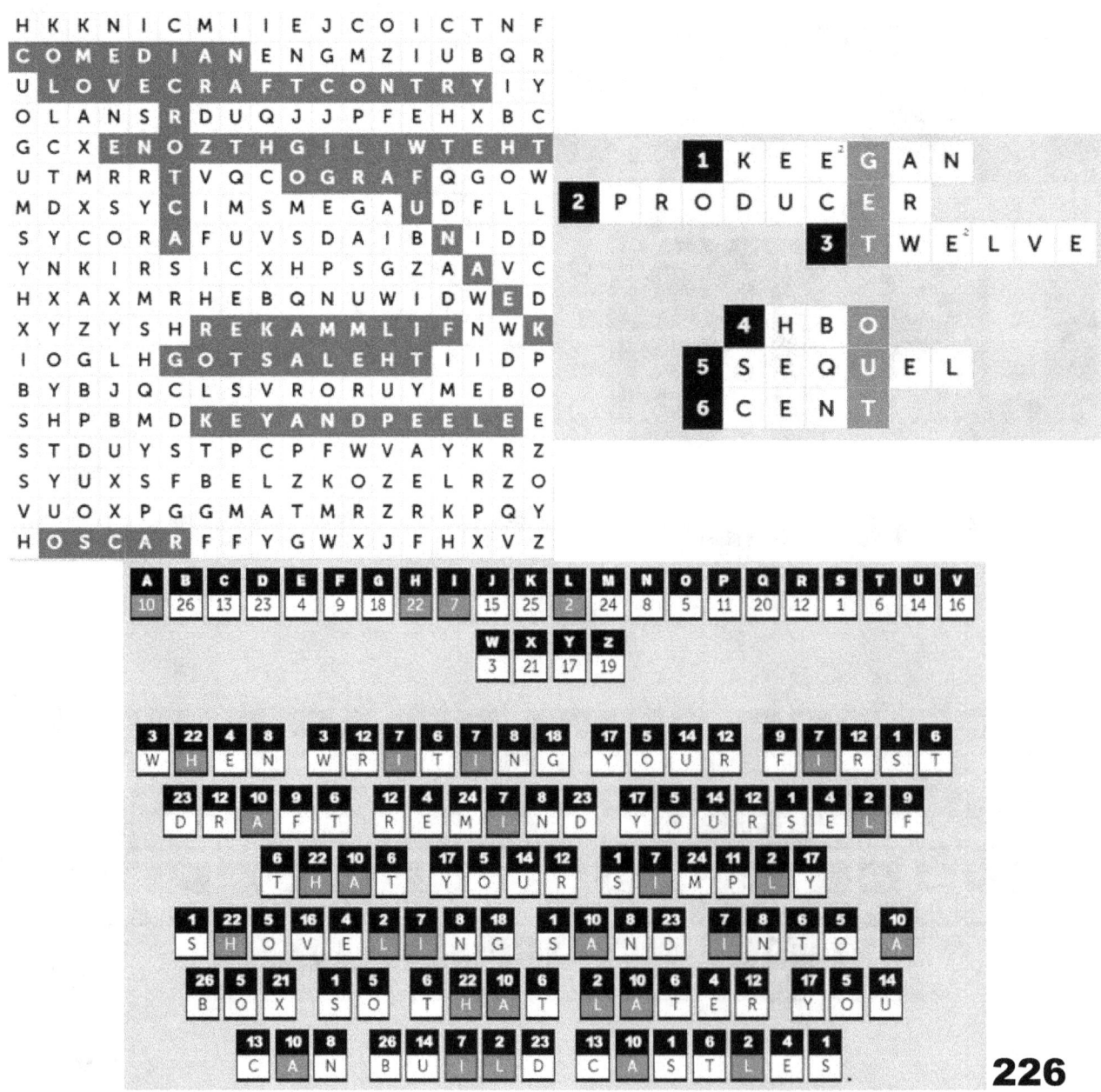

226

1. What was the name of circuit I started doing comedy?
   A. The Apollo
   B. Catch a Rising Star
   C. Cotton Club
2. What year did I get my first role in film?
   A. 1985
   B. 1987
   C. 1990
3. I wrote produced and created which show?
   A. I'm Gonna Git You Sucka
   B. The Chris Rock Show
   C. Martin

Christopher Rock
Answers

227

This book is dedicated to my grandkids
Anais Isabella Pablo-Antonio
Deyshawn Frank Chambers
Alicia Marie Jackson
Ayianna Marie Chambers
Zion Jamaris Jackson
Jayvon Jerome Jackson

ABOUT THE AUTHOR

Matthew D. Hale, the author of Black Historical Figures is a retired Marine and disabled veteran. He received his Bachelor of Arts in Computer Science from Campbell University and his Master of Science in Computer Engineering from Boston University. Matthew spends his down time making music, traveling, playing, and developing his own video games. Follow Matthew on Facebook/Meta at wegonnalearntoday, Instagram @ w_g_l_t and Tic Tok at wegonnalearntoday. Go to wegonnalearntoday.com or everydollarcountz.com for additional information.

In 2020 Matthew developed an interactive website, www.wegonnalearntoday, to provide access to Black History through games, music and videos. The website grew into the Black Historical Figures workbook series as a way to supplement the black history curricula taught in the school systems.

'In order to grow you must visit uncomfortable places'

10 BOOK SERIES
RELEASE DATES

NOVEMBER 2022

FEBRUARY 2023

MAY 2023

AUGUST 2023

NOVEMBER 2023

GET YOUR COPY TODAY
DON'T FORGET TO TELL A FRIEND

www.ingramcontent.com/pod-product-compliance
Lightning Source LLC
Chambersburg PA
CBHW080335170426
43194CB00014B/2567